D0270413

# How to Build a Computer Made Easy

Robert Penfold

Bernard Babani (publishing) Ltd
The Grampians
Shepherds Bush Road
London W6 7NF
England

0859347079

www.babanibooks.com

Bernard Babani 2009

GC 101759    GRIMSBY COLLEGE

Please note

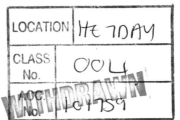

Although every care has been taken with the production of this book to ensure that any projects, designs, modifications, and/or programs, etc., contained herewith, operate in a correct and safe manner and also that any components specified are normally available in Great Britain, the Publisher and Author do not accept responsibility in any way for the failure (including fault in design) of any projects, design, modification, or program to work correctly or to cause damage to any equipment that it may be connected to or used in conjunction with, or in respect of any other damage or injury that may be caused, nor do the Publishers accept responsibility in any way for the failure to obtain specified components.

Notice is also given that if any equipment that is still under warranty is modified in any way or used or connected with home-built equipment then that warranty may be void.

© 2009 BERNARD BABANI (publishing) LTD

First Published - September 2009

British Library Cataloguing in Publication Data

A catalogue record for this book is available from the British Library

ISBN 978 0 85934 707 5

Cover Design by Gregor Arthur

Printed and bound in Great Britain for Bernard Babani (publishing) Ltd

Although assembling a PC might seem to be something that is only suitable for experts, it is really much easier than most people realise. All the parts required are available from computer shops, mail order warehouses, and computer fairs. Whether you wish to build the most budget of budget PCs, an up-market PC using the latest high-tech components, or anything in between, all the parts required are readily available.

Although one might reasonably expect building a PC to be extremely difficult, it does not require any special skills. In fact the assembly job is pretty straightforward, and it is just a matter of bolting things in place and plugging in a few cables. A crosshead screwdriver might be the only tool required, and it is unlikely that anything else apart from a pair of pliers will be needed. No soldering iron is required, and neither is any experience of electronics construction methods.

All this does not mean that PC building can be undertaken by absolutely anyone. Some experience of using and dealing with PCs is essential, and you need to be reasonably practical. Obviously some technical knowledge is needed in order to buy the right components and get everything put together properly. This book explains in simple terms exactly what components are required and how to assemble them to produce a working PC.

Having built your first PC it then requires more technical knowledge to get everything set up correctly and the operating system installed. Again, this book explains in simple terms, how to get the BIOS set up correctly. The complexity of a modern BIOS Setup program can be a bit intimidating, but in most cases it will set suitable defaults. The user just has to do little more than some "fine tuning" in order to get everything working just right. Chapter 3 explains in detail how to install and set up Windows XP, Vista, or 7, including details of any preparation needed to get the hard disc drive ready for use.

A home produced PC should have a comparable level of performance to a ready made equivalent. With wise buying it will probably cost somewhat less than a ready built PC of similar specification, although any savings are not likely to be large. However, by "rolling your own" it is possible to produce a computer that exactly meets your requirements, and you will learn a great deal in the process.  It is also good fun and should impress your friends!

*Robert Penfold*

## Trademarks

Microsoft, Windows, Windows XP, Windows Vista, and Windows 7 are either registered trademarks or trademarks of Microsoft Corporation.

All other brand and product names used in this book are recognised trademarks, or registered trademarks of their respective companies. There is no intent to use any trademarks generically and readers should investigate ownership of a trademark before using it for any purpose.

# Contents

3

# BIOS and operating system ......... 89

# Useful web addresses

These are the web addresses for some of the larger suppliers of computer components and general computer supplies. They all offer online ordering, and some have normal retail outlets as well.

| | |
|---|---|
| **Advance Tec** | **http://www.asrock.com/index.asp** |
| **Aria** | **http://www.aria.co.uk/** |
| **Dabs** | **http://www.dabs.com/** |
| **Ebuyer** | **http://www.ebuyer.com/** |
| **Maplin** | **http://www.maplin.co.uk/** |
| **Micro Direct** | **http://www.microdirect.co.uk/Home** |
| **Misco** | **http://www.misco.co.uk/** |
| **Novatech** | **http://www.novatech.co.uk/novatech/** |
| **PC World** | **http://www.pcworld.co.uk** |

These are the web addresses for most of the larger motherboard manufacturers. Motherboard manufacturer's web sites are notoriously slow, so be patient!

| | |
|---|---|
| **Abit** | **http://www.abit-usa.com/** |
| **Aopen** | **http://global.aopen.com/Products.aspx?id=52** |
| **Asrock** | **http://www.asrock.com/index.asp** |
| **Asus** | **http://uk.asus.com/** |
| **ECS Elite** | **http://www.ecsusa.com/** |
| **FIC** | **http://www.fic.com.tw/product/default.aspx** |
| **Gigabyte** | **http://www.gigabyte.com.tw/Products/Motherboard/Default.aspx** |
| **Jetway** | **http://www.jetway.com.tw/jw/** |
| **MSI** | **http://www.msicomputer.com/** |

# Overview and preparation

## Can I build it?

Constructing your own PC may seem a daunting prospect, but it is actually much easier than most people realise. It has to be emphasised that we are not talking here in terms of getting out a soldering iron and making your own motherboard, video card, etc., or even in terms of doing some metalwork to produce your own case. Due to the predominance of specialist electronic components in the PC world, most of which are not generally available, this approach is probably not viable even for those prepared to put in the massive time and effort involved. Also, by the time your completely home-made PC was finished it would probably be well and truly out of date!

What we are really talking about here is a home assembled PC based on a set of ready-made boards and housed in a commercially produced case. Everything you need to make a PC is readily available, and the tools needed to assemble one are minimal. In fact a medium size cross-point screwdriver and a pair of pliers are often the only tools required. Depending on your opinion of these things, building your own PC is as easy or as difficult as putting together your own self-assembly furniture. Inevitably there are some questions that anyone contemplating PC assembly will need answered. We will consider some of the more common questions before taking a look at the parts required and the basic steps involved in making your own PC. Construction of a PC is covered in detail in Chapter 2.

## The real thing?

Having put together your PC will it work as well as the ready-made "real thing", or will you end up with a low specification PC that is incapable of running high-end software? Provided you compare like with like there is no reason for any difference in performance and capabilities between a ready-made PC and a home-made machine. It pays to bear in mind that most PC manufacturers do not actually make their own motherboards, sound cards, etc., but instead put together PCs from "off the shelf" components. In other words, most ready-made PCs are put together in the same way as a home-made PC, and apart from the nameplate a ready-made PC is no different to a home produced equivalent.

The larger PC manufacturers often make PC components themselves or have them made to their own specification, but the underlying technology is much the same as that used in "off the shelf" components. Of course, if you put together a PC from all the cheapest parts you can lay your hands on it would be naive to expect it to equal the latest thing in commercially produced PC technology. If you build a budget PC, you will obtain budget PC performance. With computing, as with most things in life, you tend to get what you pay for.

## Will it work?

Whether you buy a PC ready-made or make it yourself it is impossible to guarantee that it will work first time and that it will continue to work flawlessly for many years. However, provided the PC is built using good quality components and you are not tempted to cut corners it should work first time. Once it is "up and running", and with average luck, it should be at least a few years before a major breakdown occurs. Obviously some constructors will have worse than average luck, and will have to deal with a fault or faults. Others will fare better than average, and will not have to fix any faults during the working life of the PC, even if it is used for many years.

Home-made and ready-made PCs should both be covered by manufacturers' warranties, but these operate in very different ways with the two types of PC. With a ready-made PC the manufacturer's guarantee should cover the PC as a whole. The manufacturer should locate the fault and fix it for you in the event that the computer does break down. There may be a return to base warranty, or some form of on-site maintenance agreement. The latter is clearly preferable to the former, but is likely to be reflected in a higher price tag for the PC, or it will be an expensive optional extra, possibly costing more than the basic price of the PC. In either case, unless you buy a lemon the time taken getting things put right should be reasonably short, and no technical skills will be required on your part.

With a home assembled PC you should have individual guarantees for every component in the system, but there is no manufacturer to provide an overall guarantee for the complete PC. If something goes wrong it is up to you to find out just what has gone awry and get the faulty component exchanged under warranty. Locating the faulty component is not usually too difficult, but getting it replaced quickly is not always possible. If the faulty component was ordered by mail order you will have to send it back, it is likely that it will then go through some sort of testing, and then the replacement will be sent. This could leave the PC out of action for several days. Of course, if you buy a ready-made PC by mail order and it has a return to base warranty, you have the same problem. In fact matters are worse because the whole PC often has to be returned, not just the faulty component.

This lack of speed in getting things fixed may or may not matter. Where it is important to get a PC working straight away, and to keep it working, a ready-made PC with an on-site maintenance agreement with a reputable company is the safest option. You have no absolute guarantee of quick fixes, but there is a good chance of keeping any downtimes to a minimum. You may find a company prepared to offer on-site maintenance on a home constructed PC, but this is very unlikely.

There can be odd hardware or software incompatibility problems, and these tend to be difficult to solve whether you buy a ready-made PC or build one yourself. Whoever you complain to, it is always the other company's fault! Fortunately, this type of thing is much rarer than it used to be, and it is probably not a major issue any more. These incompatibility problems are usually the result of faults in one of the device drivers rather than a problem with the hardware itself. Improved drivers usually appear on the manufacturer's web site before too long.

## Will I save money?

Many people try their hand at DIY PC construction in an attempt to save money. Provided you purchase the individual components wisely it is likely that there will be a small cost saving. However, do not expect to get a half price PC by building it yourself. A saving of around 10 percent is certainly quite possible, and with careful buying of "special offers" you may even achieve a saving of as much as 20 percent or so. On the other hand, with imprudent buying you could easily end up paying 10 or 20 percent more for your PC. Assembling a PC takes no more than a very few hours work, and it would be unrealistic to expect the DIY approach to produce massive cost savings.

It is probably not the assembly costs that account for the majority of the savings anyway. When you buy a new PC it generally comes complete with some form of support package such as a one-year onsite maintenance contract and some sort of telephone support system. With a home produced PC you have to be more self-sufficient. There may well be telephone or Email support for some of the components, but in general it is up to you to sort things out when problems arise.

If you are able to sort out these problems yourself it makes sense to do so rather than pay for support that you do not really need, and will probably never use. Looking at things the other way, if your experience with PCs is strictly limited, building your own PC is probably not a good idea. Should things go wrong, your chances of sorting them out would also be strictly limited.

## Can I do it?

As pointed out previously, actually putting the computer together does not require a great deal of skill. Someone who is completely impractical would be well advised not to attempt building a PC, or anything else for that matter. You should be able to physically put the PC together provided you are not a DIY disaster waiting to happen. This is not to say that anyone who can use a screwdriver is properly qualified to build a PC. When dealing with computers odd little problems tend to develop, particularly when dealing with device drivers and software installation.

As pointed out previously, someone with a few years experience of using PCs should be able to sort out these problems without too much difficulty. For "old hands" at computing this sort of thing is just part of the fun. For a newcomer to PCs it could be difficult and time consuming to get the finished product set up and really working well. In fact it could be difficult to get the PC set up and working at all. Consequently, I would only recommend PC assembly if you have had a few years experience with PCs and are not going to panic if minor problems occur.

## Why bother?

If constructing your own PC is not going to save large amounts of money, and you will have to sort out any minor problems yourself, why bother? Although any savings in cost are not likely to be huge, a worthwhile saving can still be made. Alternatively, for the same money it should be possible to produce a PC with a higher specification by doing it yourself.

However, for most constructors the main motivation is not saving money or obtaining a bigger and better PC. Many people find that making their own PC is a fun and interesting experience in its own right. If you like making things, having built one PC it is unlikely that you will return to the world of ready-made PCs. I suppose that for many people the kudos of building your own PC is another plus point. It is a good way to impress your friends.

For most PC builders the main advantage is that you can build a PC having the exact specification you require. Many PC companies will to some extent customise one of their standard PCs to suit your requirements, but few will build one to your exact specification. Where such a facility is offered, it is often quite expensive, as one would probably expect for a bespoke service.

By doing it yourself you can have the video and soundcards you deem the best, the most suitable monitor for your requirements, and so on. If you only need a small hard disc drive but need an advanced 3D-video card and large monitor, then that is what you buy. The time you save in searching for a PC with the right specification at the right price should be more than enough to build the PC yourself. Financial constraints may force a few compromises, but you should end up with the best possible PC for your requirements, or something as near to it as the available money permits.

Another potential advantage of building your own is that it may be possible to use parts from your previous PC. Being realistic about it, there will probably be few (if any) original parts from a really old PC that will be suitable for use in a new one. A few items such as the mouse, keyboard, and floppy disc drive will probably be usable if they are in good condition, but little else is likely to be of much use. However, most PCs get a certain amount of upgrading over the years, and any recent additions to the old PC will probably be usable in the new one. For example, a recently added DVD or CD-RW drive, sound card, or loudspeaker system is usually suitable for transplanting into a new PC. Again, the saving in cost is not likely to be huge, but the cost of the new PC can be significantly reduced without severely compromising its performance.

The situation is rosier if you tend to switch to a new computer relatively often. In an extreme case it could just be a matter of replacing the existing motherboard, processor, and memory, with the rest of the computer being left untouched. I suppose that this type of thing should really be classified as rebuilding or upgrading rather than building a PC. Where you have an existing PC that is proving to be a bit slow, this type of rebuild or

*Fig.1.1 A DVD drive, such as this DVD writer, is an essential item*

upgrade will often provide the cheapest way of moving up to a PC having an adequate specification for your purposes. However, do not overlook the possibility of building a new PC "from scratch" and keeping the existing PC as a standby, giving it to the children, or otherwise continuing to use it. It is wasteful if you discard PC components that still have years of life left in them.

One final point that is worth making is that you will learn a great deal about PCs by building your own. Constructing a PC will not turn you into a computer expert overnight, but you will certainly learn a great deal about the way everything functions. If any problems arise in the future or you wish to upgrade a PC it should be much easier to sort things out once you have some experience of PC construction.

## Getting started

Having decided to "take the plunge" and build your own PC the first task is to make a list of all the components required, complete with brief notes detailing any special requirements. You may already have a fair idea of what you require, but otherwise it is a matter of studying reviews in computer magazines and looking through magazine advertisements in order to find the best components at a price you can afford.

If your aim is merely to produce a PC at a "rock bottom" price it becomes more a matter of scanning the advertisements for "special offers" and touring the local computer fairs for the best deals you can obtain. Before buying any "bargain" components make sure that they are compatible with the other items in the system, and are not totally out of date. Be particularly wary of very cheap motherboards, as these often require obsolete processors and memory modules that can cost a great deal and give relatively poor performance. If components are offered at very low prices there is usually a catch somewhere.

This list represents the minimum you will require in order to produce a working PC.

- Case with PSU (power supply unit), set of fixings, etc.

- Motherboard ("mobo" or main board) with cables, etc.

- Memory modules to suit the motherboard

- Microprocessor with matching heatsink and fan

- Keyboard and mouse

- Video card

- Monitor

- Hard disc drive

- DVD drive

The above list omits some items that most PC users will require, such as a printer and a modem, but here we will only consider the main constituent parts of the PC itself. It is advisable to put together a basic PC and get it working, and then add peripherals such as scanners, printers, and broadband modems. Most people who build their own PC already have many of these peripherals anyway.

A floppy disc drive used to be an essential component, since it was needed in order to set up the hard disc drive and install the operating system. Things moved on, and it became possible to prepare the hard disc drive and install the operating system from a CD-ROM. Now things have moved on further still, and it is actually a DVD drive that is needed in order to install Windows. Any setting up of the hard disc is carried out as part of the Windows installation process. A DVD reader is all that is needed, but drives that can read and write to a wide range of CD and DVD media are quite cheap these days, so one of these DVD writers is a better choice (Figure 1.1).

DVD and CD drives are available in various colours, so it is usually possible to buy one that matches the colour of the case. Obviously this might not be possible if you opt for one of the more "way out" cases in something like fluorescent green or day-glow orange. These days it is increasingly common for CD and DVD drives to be supplied with alternative bezels (Figure 1.2) so that you can use the one that best matches the exterior finish of the case.

## Integrated audio/video

For multimedia applications, voice recognition, etc., you will also require a sound card and speakers plus (possibly) a headset and microphone. For most purposes one of the budget audio cards will suffice. A fair proportion of current motherboards have built-in audio circuits that offer a reasonable range of features and performance. In fact some of these integral sound facilities are very sophisticated, providing various forms of surround-sound. Integrated audio is probably the best option unless a top-notch audio system is required for some reason. There seems to be little difference in the cost of a motherboard having built-in audio and one having similar features but no integral audio. Integrated audio is therefore very cost-effective.

These days a fair proportion of motherboards have integrated video circuits. Whether integrated video is worthwhile depends on the way in which the PC will be used. It is unlikely that the performance of integrated video will satisfy dedicated computer gamers. In order to get the best results from the latest games it is necessary to have a high quality 3D video card that has all the latest tricks. For those not primarily interested in games it is quite possible that the integrated approach will be perfectly adequate.

The built-in video circuits have some 3D capability, incidentally, but obviously they do not rival expensive video cards that cost substantially more than a motherboard with an integrated video facility. Integrated video is generally regarded as more than adequate for a PC that will only be used to run business applications and the like. With a modern

*Fig.1.2  For the colour conscious, alternative bezels are sometimes
         provided*

motherboard it should also be up to the task of playing DVDs and
performing other multimedia tasks.

Integrated video, like integrated audio, is very cost effective. It is therefore
a good choice when building a budget PC. However, bear in mind that
most built-in video circuits share the main system memory. If (say) 128
megabytes of memory are used for the video generator, there are 128
megabytes less for everything else. This can slow down the PC slightly
unless extra memory is fitted. As memory is now relatively cheap and
most new PCs are equipped with large amounts of it, this is perhaps less
of a problem than it was a few years ago. However, it is something to
bear in mind if you will use an integrated video system in its most
advanced modes together with an operating system that requires large
amounts of memory in order to work well.

## Right price?

Having selected the components for your new PC it is time to add up the
cost. This tends to be higher than you would expect, so it may be
necessary to come up with some extra money or compromise slightly
and choose some cheaper components. It is also worth looking through

some catalogues and magazine adverts to see if you can find better deals on some of the components. However, most of the best deals tend to be available on the Internet, so a little research online is likely to produce the lowest prices for your selected components.

It is essential to make sure that the components will actually fit together to produce a working PC. There are more options available than in days gone by, which means that there are also more opportunities for hardware incompatibility to creep in. The main board, for example, will be designed to work with certain sizes and types of memory, and with a certain range of processors. It is likely that the finished computer will not work if you simply choose a motherboard that has the features you require and then add your selected processor. In fact it might not even be possibly to physically fit the processor onto the motherboard. Hardware compatibility is a subject that is covered in more detail in subsequent sections of this chapter.

# Case and PSU

As when buying a new PC, various sizes and styles of case are available. It is a matter of choosing whichever style best fits into your particular set-up, but when building your first PC it is probably a good idea to avoid any of the more unusual types such as very compact cases. Construction is likely to be easiest using something "run of the mill" such as a desktop, mini tower, or midi tower case.

The mini tower option gives a relatively small and neat end result, but you need to make sure that a case of this type will actually accommodate everything. There should be no problem in fitting the motherboard into a mini tower case if one of the smaller types is used, but a full-size motherboard might not be a very practical choice for a small case, if it will actually fit in at all. With a full-size motherboard I would definitely opt for a slightly larger case, such as a midi tower or desktop type. When building your first PC it is definitely advisable not to choose one of the really small cases or any other unusual types.

A lack of drive bays is a more likely cause of problems with a small case. A PC case has two sizes of drive bays (Figure 1.3). The smaller bays take 3.5-inch drives such as a 3.5-inch floppy disc drive and most hard drives. The larger bays (the ones at the top in Figure 1.3) are the 5.25-inch variety and take CD-ROM drives, DVD writers, etc. These days many PCs are equipped with a built-in memory card reader that can be used with various types of Flash memory card (CF SD, XC, etc.). These fit into a drive bay, and they are widely available in 3.5-inch and 5.25-inch types.

Usually one or more of the 3.5-inch drive bays do not have cut-outs in the front panel. These are used for hard disc drives, which do not have to be externally accessible. Since floppy disc drives are now often omitted from PCs, not every PC case actually has any 3.5-inch drive bays that are externally accessible. However, there are other accessories that require 3.5-inch bays that are accessible, such as the control panels of some sound systems and Flash card readers mentioned previously. Consequently, a case that has externally accessible 3.5-inch bays is more versatile and is perhaps a better choice.

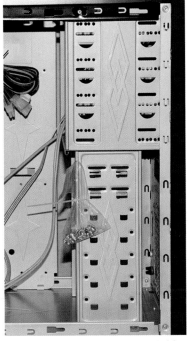

*Fig.1.3  There are two sizes of drive bay*

A mini tower can usually accommodate more hard disc drives than you are ever likely to install in one PC, and it is the externally accessible drive bays that tend to be the limiting factor. There should be no problem if you use something like a single DVD writer and one hard disc drive. Things are more likely to be problematic if the PC will be equipped with something more like two DVD writers, a built-in Flash card reader, a 3.5-inch floppy disc drive, and a couple of hard disc drives. Many mini tower cases lack the external drive bays needed for this configuration, and a midi tower or desktop case would probably be a more practical choice.

PC cases are often supplied complete with a power supply unit, but this is not always the case, so it is best to check this point before you part with any money. As one would probably expect, the power supplies included with low-cost cases are usually of the "cheap and cheerful" variety. The power ratings are sometimes a bit optimistic, and the noise produced by the cooling fan tends to be too loud to permit the completed PC to be used in media applications. In fact some of the power supplies

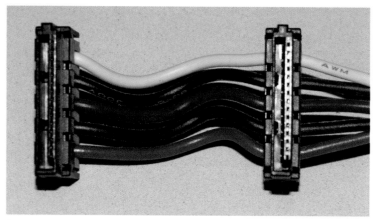

*Fig.1.4  A power supply lead with two SATA power connectors*

included with the more upmarket cases are irritatingly loud. It is probably worth trying the power supply included with a case, but it would be prudent to budget for a higher quality low-noise type in case the supplied unit proves to be not good enough.

## Getting connected

PC power supplies have a wattage rating, and this must be high enough to accommodate everything in the computer. It is reasonable to ask the minimum rating that will suffice, but this is very much a "how long is a piece of string" sort of question. It depends on factors such as the number and type of drives fitted in the computer, the type of processor and its speed, etc.

In general, a 450 watt power supply is adequate for a PC that has a fairly average specification, but something more beefy such as a 650 or 750 watt unit would be required for a PC that has more drives than usual, a powerful graphics card, or some other form of power-hungry hardware. As pointed out previously, the ratings of the power supplies included with cheap cases are often a bit over-optimistic, and the same is true of very low cost power supplies obtained separately. It is worth paying a bit extra for a supply that will run quietly and at full specification.

In order to be fully usable it is essential that the power supply has sufficient connectors of the right types to properly accommodate the motherboard

*Fig.1.5  The large connector on this DVD drive actually consists of separate power and data ports*

and drives.  There are three types of power connector used for drives, and the power supply should have all three types.  There will probably be just one 3.5-inch power connector, and these are only used for 3.5-inch floppy disc drives.  Consequently, in a modern PC this connector is often left unused.

There are usually two or more of the larger 5.25-inch connectors, which were originally used for 5.25-inch floppy disc drives.  These days they are used for parallel IDE drives, such as some DVD and hard disc drives.  However, parallel IDE drives are being phased out in favour of the relatively new serial (SATA) type.  Some serial drives have provision for the old type of power connector, but this is a rarity these days.  Therefore, the 5.25-inch power connectors might also be unnecessary in a new PC.

Modern hard disc drives and DVD drives use a SATA interface, and have a SATA power connector.  This requires the appropriate type of power connector on the PSU drive leads, and a PSU lead fitted with two SATA power connectors is shown in Figure 1.4.  The rear of a SATA drive (Figure 1.5) can give the impression that there is just one large connector, but the single large connector is actually two sockets.  The larger one on the left is the power port, and the smaller one on the right is for the data cable.

*Fig.1.6  A supply splitter.  This one uses a 5.25-inch connector on the
       input side, but a SATA version is also available*

Anyway, a minimum of two SATA power connectors are required, with
one being needed for the hard disc and the other being required for the
DVD drive.  If you decide to have one or two additional drives it will be
necessary to have three or four SATA power connectors.  Unfortunately,
many of the PC power supplies being sold at present are a bit behind
the times, and have just one SATA power lead.

This does not make them unusable in a modern PC, but it does mean
that one or more adaptors will be needed in order to provide power to all
the drives.  Several types of adaptor are available, including one that
converts a 5.25-inch power connector to a SATA type, and a similar type
for 3.5-inch power leads is also produced.  Another way of providing
additional SATA power leads is to use a splitter (Figure 1.6).  This connects
to a power lead from the PSU and provides two SATA power leads that
connect to the drives.

Many PCs now have a built-in memory card reader fitted in one of the
drive bays.  On the face of it, a built-in card reader will use one of the
power supply's power leads.  This is not usually the case though, since
integral card readers, like the external variety, connect to a USB port.
They obtain their power from this port, and no separate power lead is
needed.

## Processor and motherboard

All modern PCs are based on an Intel Pentium processor, or a compatible
processor from another manufacturer.  These days the only real
competition to Intel is provided by AMD with their very popular Sempron,
Athlon, and Phenom processor ranges.  Pentium processors have
additional instructions, but are basically just faster and more efficient
versions of the 80486DX and earlier Intel processors in this series.  It is

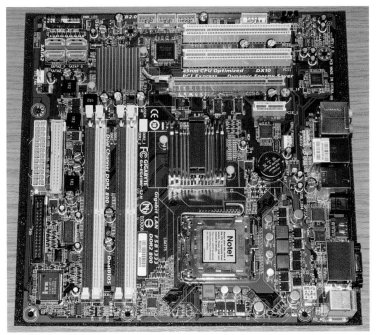

*Fig.1.7  A motherboard for Intel processors that has integrated sound
and graphics*

important to know from the outset that you cannot simply choose a
processor, then choose a motherboard that has the right features at a
good price, and then expect the two to work together perfectly.  You
either have to choose a processor and then select a suitable motherboard
for that processor, or choose a motherboard and then select a compatible
processor.  I suppose that it is more a matter of finding some likely
processor and motherboard combinations that are within your budget,
and then choosing the combination that best suits your needs.

The main reason that you cannot select the motherboard and processor
in isolation is that the Intel and AMD ranges are incompatible.  They both
run the same operating systems and application software, and in that
sense they are compatible.  However, they are physically and electrically
incompatible, and a motherboard can only use one make of processor
or the other.  Another point to bear in mind is that compatibility with your
selected make of processor does not mean that the motherboard will be
able to use any processor from that manufacturer.

It is essential to check that the selected motherboard is compatible with the processor that you intend to use with it. This is especially important when using a processor that is fairly new to the market. Older motherboard designs are often incapable of using the latest processors. Motherboard manufacturer's web sites usually provide a full list of compatible processors for each of their motherboards. With most motherboards it is possible to download the instruction manual from the manufacturer's website. This provides detailed information about the board, including all the ports it provides, the type or types of memory supported, and so on. I never buy any motherboard until I have downloaded and read through the instruction manual.

Unless you will be running applications that genuinely need separate sound and graphics systems, having these functions integrated with the motherboard is the neatest and cheapest solution. Integrated sound and video facilities can usually be switched off via the BIOS Setup program, so it should still be possible to upgrade either. A modern budget or mid-range motherboard should provide good performance and a reasonable range of features, so there is no point in buying an upmarket type unless you really need the additional features it provides. Figure 1.7 shows the motherboard used in the demonstration PC that forms the basis of Chapter 2. This has integrated sound, graphics, and has numerous ports. It has four expansion ports, but these may never be needed.

## Processor advice

The range of processors currently available is a bit bewildering, and seems to get ever more diverse. It can be difficult to decide which one is the most suitable for a given set of circumstances. Unless money is not an issue it is probably best not to opt for the last word in PC microprocessors. When 66MHz 80486DX microprocessors became available they were only 33MHz faster than the existing 33MHz chips, but that 33MHz represented a doubling in speed. A 3GHz chip is 200MHz faster than a 2.8GHz version, but offers an increase in performance of just a few percent. Even going from a 2.4GHz processor to a 3GHz type only represents a 25 percent increase.

Even with the more demanding applications software an increase in speed of a few percent will be barely noticeable. Programs that run slowly on a 2.8GHz PC will still run slowly on a 3GHz PC. Where there is a minimal difference in cost it might be worthwhile going for the slightly faster version of a processor, particularly if you are running processor intensive applications, but otherwise it does not make economic sense to do so. The situation is complicated by the fact that some processors achieve far more per clock cycle than do others. Bear in mind that other factors, such as the amount and type of memory, can also have a major influence on the speed at which a computer will run a given application.

Price is usually a good indication of relative processing power. At the budget end of the market there are modern but relatively simple processors, and older designs that are now being sold at a fraction of their original price. Older processors can offer excellent performance at low cost, but only if the motherboard and memory can be obtained at equally attractive prices. Bear in mind that a new PC that uses relatively old technology is unlikely to be particularly future-proof. You are effectively building a PC that is a few years old.

Going up in price, you then have a choice of mid-range modern processors and upmarket processors that are beginning to become a bit dated. In general, mid-priced processors are safe choices that offer good performance for the money, and do not require the latest mega-powerful (and expensive) motherboards and memory. In contrast, top end processors tend to be very expensive, require expensive motherboards and other components in order to work really well, and do not represent good value for money. Obtaining the last word in PC computing power is an expensive business, and the additional cost is often out of proportion to the increase in performance over mid-range options.

## Intel or AMD?

Once a price range has been selected, a choice of Intel or AMD has to be made, and it pays to bear in mind that these use different motherboards. At one time the motherboards for Intel chips tended to be significantly more expensive than those for AMD processors. These days there is little difference in the prices of the two types, and the facilities offered by the motherboard is the main factor governing the price. In general, AMD processors cost slightly less than Intel types for a given level of performance. Therefore, when operating on a tight budget it is still a good idea to consider various processor and motherboard options, and to take into account the cost of different types of memory. Provided the rest of the system is up to the task, any AMD or Intel processor should provide excellent results together with good reliability.

Buying a fast processor and then economising on the rest of the system does not usually produce the best system for the money. Many applications programs will run better with a slightly slower processor plus more memory and a better video card. Overall results are likely to be best with a well balanced system that has no major weaknesses.

Even the cheapest of the current budget processors are adequate for most business and general applications. Many of these applications require large amounts of memory though, as does multitasking (running several programs simultaneously). Windows Vista and 7 tend to require more memory than Windows XP, and it is especially important to bear this in mind when building a PC that will run Windows Vista. A gigabyte of memory is the absolute minimum for good results, and 2 gigabytes or more is preferable. Skimping on the memory to pay for an expensive processor is usually a mistake. Skimping slightly on the processor to fit more memory is often the better strategy.

## Heatsink and fan

The original PC processors managed quite happily without any cooling system, but all modern PC processors are short lived unless they are kept cool by a heatsink and fan. A heatsink is simply a piece of metal having fins that enable it to efficiently transfer excess heat from the processor to the air inside the case. The cooling fan improves the efficiency of the heatsink by ensuring that there is a flow of cool air over it.

These days the heatsink and fan are invariably in the form of a single unit, and you do not buy them as separate entities. In fact processors are sometimes supplied as a sort of boxed set, complete with heatsink, fan, and fitting instructions, so you may not need to buy the heatsink and fan separately. This is the safe way to obtain the heatsink and fan, as they are guaranteed to be a correct match for the processor. Processors offered at "rock bottom" prices are usually the OEM (original equipment manufacturer) versions, which are "bare" processors with no heatsink and fan.

When buying the heatsink and fan it is important to realise that there are different sizes and types. The Socket AM2 uses a totally different method of fixing to the Socket 775 types, and consequently needs a totally different heatsink and fan. Some processors generate more heat than others, and therefore need a larger heatsink. Other than buying them as a boxed set, the safest way to buy the heatsink and fan is to obtain them from the same source as the processor and at the same time, preferably getting an assurance that the cooling system is suitable for use with the processor. Any company selling processors should be able to supply a matching heatsink and fan.  If anything should go wrong any reputable company should be prepared to make amends for their mistake.

## Motherboard

Having selected the processor it is then a matter of finalising the choice of motherboard.  As explained previously, AMD and Intel processors use different motherboards, so do not waste time looking at boards that are totally incompatible with your chosen processor.  When you find some likely looking motherboards it is essential to carefully check their specifications to ascertain whether or not they will accept the processor you intend to use.

Also as pointed out previously, it is worthwhile investigating the web sites of some motherboard manufacturers.  These sites usually contain a great deal of technical information on the motherboards produced by each manufacturer, and there are often charts to show the processors that are compatible with each board.  Where possible, download the full instruction manuals for any boards that are of interest.  Apart from helping you to select a suitable motherboard, reading through a few of these manuals can teach you a great deal about PC building and setting up the finished unit.

All modern motherboards are of the ATX variety, and the earlier AT boards are now long gone.   There are some variations within the ATX scheme of things, and if you look at a few ATX boards it will soon become apparent that they are produced in various shapes and sizes.  They all fit into the same cases though, and are used in much the same way.  The differences are due to the fact that technology has enabled modern motherboards to be made much smaller than those of a few years ago, despite the fact that the current boards are much more complex.

Rather than produce full-size boards that are largely blank, the manufacturers have opted to make boards that are half size, or whatever. A wide variety of layouts are currently in use, and some are very easy to use.  With others you tend to find that some of the connectors are a bit inaccessible once the board is mounted in the case.  In general, small boards are easier to use, but the small size is often reflected in a more limited range of facilities and expansion potential.

## Memory

Various types of memory have been used in PCs over the years, but modern motherboards use some form of DDR (double data rate) memory

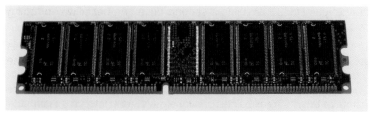

*Fig.1.8 A DDR memory module*

modules. In addition to the original DDR modules (Figure 1.8) there are now the improved DDR2 and DDR3 varieties. Each type is available in various operating speeds. It is essential to check which types and speeds are compatible with the motherboard and processor combination you will be using. The motherboard's instruction manual should provide the information you require.

In the past it was often necessary to use memory modules in pairs, but modern motherboards are generally more accommodating. However, in order to obtain optimum performance it might still be necessary to use pairs of modules in dual channel operation. Again, the motherboard's instruction manual should clarify the situation. Bear in mind that an ordinary 32-bit version of Windows will only be able to use about 3 to 3.5 gigabytes of memory, so there is no point in fitting more than this unless you intend to use a 64-bit operating system.

With the current low cost of PC memory, there is probably no point in using less than about 2 gigabytes of memory. With memory modules it is probably best not to use the cheapest type you can find. Past (and often bitter) experience with memory products suggests that it is worth paying a little extra to obtain modules produced by one of the well-known manufacturers.

## Drives

Modern motherboards usually have provision for parallel IDE hard disc drives, and the serial (SATA) type. However, the parallel interfaces are really only included for use with DVD drives and for optimum performance SATA hard disc drives should be used. There is nothing to stop you from using a parallel hard disc drive if (say) you wish to use a drive removed from a PC that is being scrapped. Bear in mind though, that using and old parallel IDE drive in an otherwise up-to-date PC could significantly reduce its performance. Using a new SATA main drive and the old parallel IDE drive as a second drive is a better way of doing things.

There is a second and faster version of the SATA interface, which is called SATA2. All modern motherboards and hard disc drives have the new version of the SATA interface. It is possible to use a SATA drive with a motherboard that has SATA2 interfaces, but the speed of data transfers will be at the lower rate dictated by the drive, and not at the faster rate available from the motherboard. Using an old SATA drive in a modern PC will actually produce a very respectable level of performance, but it is clearly not a good way of doing things if you are trying to build a very fast PC.

As explained previously, modern versions of Windows are supplied on a DVD, and a drive that can read DVDs is an essential feature. Without one it is not possible to install Windows on a standalone PC. Modern CD-ROM and DVD drives have a SATA interface, but an old parallel IDE drive should work well enough should you wish to use one from a defunct PC. A floppy disc drive is no longer needed in order to install the operating system, so do not bother with one of these unless you are still using floppy discs. If you use any form of Flash memory card it is well worthwhile fitting your new PC with an integral card reader.

## Video card

It will be necessary to buy a video card if a motherboard having integrated graphics does not provide the required level of video performance. AGP cards are now obsolete, and it will therefore be a 16X PCI Express card that is needed. Any modern motherboard should have an expansion slot of this type, but is unlikely to have an AGP type as well. Using an AGP video card from a PC that is being scrapped will probably not be an option. Using an old video card might be a bit pointless anyway, since it might not give better performance than modern integrated graphics. Boards that have integrated graphics can usually accept a PCI Express video card, so you can build a PC having relatively simple integrated graphics and then update to an "all singing, all dancing" video board later on.

## Keyboard and mouse

Some motherboards have the old PS/2 mouse and keyboard connectors, and can therefore be used with PS/2 and USB types. However, not all modern motherboards have PS/2 ports, so it is as well to check this

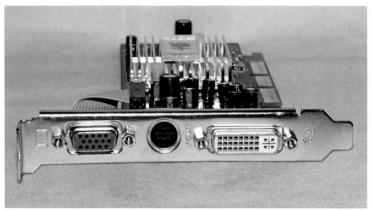

*Fig.1.9 This video card has an ordinary VGA output (left) and a DVI
type (right)*

point before buying the keyboard and mouse, although most modern
keyboards and mice are of the USB variety, or have an adaptor that
enables them to be used with PS/2 or USB ports.

A problem is more likely to occur if you try to use an old keyboard and
mouse with the new PC. Many people get used to a particular keyboard
and mouse, and like to go on using them when switching to a new PC.
Should you wish to use an old PS/2 keyboard or mouse with a new PC
that does not have suitable ports, all is not lost. It is possible to obtain an
inexpensive adaptor that uses a USB port to provide PS/2 mouse and
keyboard ports.

## Monitor

When buying a monitor it used to be a matter of spending a substantial
amount of money to obtain a monitor that was expensive to run and
provided mediocre results. LCD technology has transformed the monitor
market, and these days you can obtain a good 22-inch widescreen
monitor for under a hundred pounds. The running costs are only a fraction
of those associated with the CRT monitors of the past, and the picture
quality is usually of a standard that we could only have dreamt about
until a few years ago.

What constitutes the best monitor is very much a personal choice, so it
is preferable to see some likely candidates in action before making a
choice. For some reason the default settings of most monitors seem to

provide such high levels of brightness and contrast that the picture is barely usable. Consequently, it is a good idea to try adjusting the controls to optimise the picture quality before deciding whether a monitor is to your liking.

There are two common types of interface used with PC monitors, and the 15-pin VGA type is the one that has been in common use for many years. The DVI (digital video interface) is relatively new, but is now in widespread use. Most video cards have VGA and DVI outputs (Figure 1.9), but integrated graphics are often limited to just the old VGA type. It used to be rare for monitors to have DVI inputs, and those that did were relatively expensive. This is no longer the case, and there are plenty of mid-price and even budget monitors that sport this feature. An ordinary VGA input is normally included as well.

In theory, using a DVI interface provides the best results. In practice there is normally little or no discernible difference, but where both types of interface are available on the monitor and the computer I suppose it makes sense to use the DVI interface. The important thing is to make sure that the computer and the monitor have a common interface that enables them to be connected together. Note that monitors do not always come complete with a data cable for the connection to the computer. Where a lead is included, it is usually a VGA type and not a DVI type. If you use the DVI interface it will probably be necessary to buy a DVI cable separately. Unfortunately, this type of computer lead is one of the more expensive types.

## Protection racket

Before starting assembly, or even touching any of the components, it is important to understand the risk of damaging electronic components with discharges of static electricity. I think it is worth making the point that it does not take a large static charge complete with sparks and "cracking" sounds to damage sensitive electronic components. Large static discharges of that type are sufficient to damage most semiconductor components, and not just the more sensitive ones.

Many of the components used in computing are so sensitive to static charges that they can be damaged by relatively small voltages. These charges will not generate noticeable sparks or make your hair stand on end, but they are nevertheless harmful to many electronic components. Hence you can "zap" these components simply by touching them, and in most cases would not be aware that anything had happened.

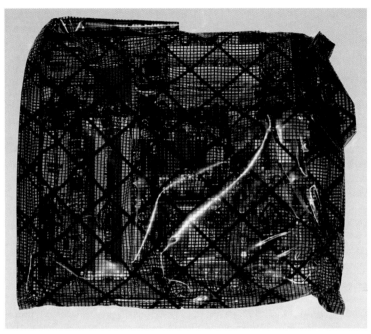

*Fig.1.10  A motherboard in its conductive plastic bag*

I think it is also worth making the point that it is not just the processor and memory modules that are vulnerable.  Completed circuit boards such as video and soundcards are often vulnerable to static damage, as is the motherboard itself.  In fact most modern expansion cards and all motherboards are vulnerable to damage from static charges.  Even components such as the hard disc drive and CD-ROM drive can be damaged by static charges.  The case and power supply assembly plus any heatsinks and cooling fans represent the only major components that you can assume to be zap-proof.  Everything else should be regarded as potentially at risk and handled accordingly.

When handling any vulnerable computer components you should always keep well away from any known or likely sources of static electricity.  These includes such things as computer monitors, television sets, any carpets or furnishings that are known to be prone to static generation, and even any pets that are known to get charged-up fur coats.  In general, objects that are wholly or partly made from metal are safer than those that are made entirely from plastic.

Avoid wearing any clothes that are known to give problems with static charges. This seems to be less of a problem than it once was, because few clothes these days are made from a cloth that consists entirely of man-made fibres. There is normally a significant content of natural fibres, and this seems to be sufficient to prevent any significant build-up of static charges. However, if you should have any garments that might give problems, make sure that you do not wear them when handling any computer equipment or components.

When you obtain the components for a PC it is tempting to unpack them all and have a good look at all the items you have purchased. This is not really a good idea though, since most of the components will be in some form of anti-static packing. In the example of Figure 1.10 the motherboard is in an antic-static bag that is made from conductive plastic, and this is probably the most common form of anti-static packing used for computer parts. Components should be safe while in the special packing, but will be vulnerable as soon as they are removed from it. The components should only be handled under safe conditions.

## Anti-static equipment

Electronics and computing professionals often use quite expensive equipment to ensure that static charges are kept at bay. Most of these are not practical propositions for amateur computer enthusiasts or those who only deal with computers professionally on a very part-time basis. If you will only be working on computers from time to time, some inexpensive anti-static equipment is all that you need to ensure that there are no expensive accidents.

When working on a motherboard it is essential to have some form of conductive worktop that is earthed. These can be purchased from the larger electronic component suppliers, but something as basic as a large sheet of aluminium cooking foil laid out on the workbench will do the job very well. The only slight problem is that some way of earthing the foil must be devised.

The method I generally adopt is to connect the foil to the metal chassis of a computer using a crocodile clip lead. Crocodile clips are available from electronic component suppliers, as are sets of made-up leads. The ready-made leads are often quite short, but several can be clipped together to make up a longer lead. The computer that acts as the earth must be plugged into the mains supply so that it is earthed via the mains earth lead. The computer **should be switched off**, and the supply should

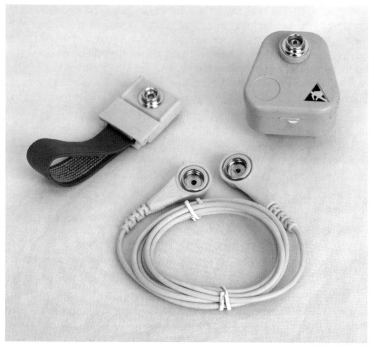

*Fig.1.11  A conductive wristband with its lead and earthing plug.  This
is an essential piece of equipment*

also be **switched off at the mains socket**.  The earth lead is never
switched, and the case will remain earthed even when the computer is
switched off.

You can make quite sure that your body remains static-free by earthing
yourself using a proper earthing wristband.  This is basically just a
wristband made from electrically conductive material that connects to
the earth via a lead and a high value resistor.  The resistor does not
prevent any static build-up in your body from leaking away to earth, but
it will protect you from a significant shock if a fault should result in the
earthing point becoming "live".

There are two ways of earthing the wristband.  One of these is to have a
crocodile clip on the end of the earthing lead, and this can be connected
to any piece of earthed metal that happens to be handy.  In a PC context
this usually means the chassis of a PC, but there might be other electrical

gadgets having earthed chassis that could be used. The easier method, and the one I would recommend, is to have a sort of dummy mains plug on the earthing lead (Figure 1.11). This enables the wristband to be earthed via any mains socket, which should be **switched off**.

Of course, only the earth pin of the plug connects to the wristband, and the rest of the plug is normally plastic so that there is no risk of a fault causing the wristband to be connected to a "live" pin. The resistor is included in the lead, so there is no danger of receiving a strong electric shock if, for instance, the mains socket's wiring is faulty.

Note that anti-static wrist-bands are sometimes sold as a complete kit with everything you need, but they are also sold as individual items (wristband, lead, and earthing plug or clip). Make sure that you know exactly what you are buying before parting with any money. Even if you are intending to do no more than very occasional PC building, upgrading, or servicing, a good quality wristband kit should be regarded as an essential item of equipment. It will ensure that you can handle computer components safely for many years.

## Assembly

I suppose there is no single right way of assembling a PC, but there is usually a certain order of assembly that is easier and more efficient than the alternatives. The best order might vary somewhat depending on the particular case, motherboard, and drives used, so the general scheme of things suggested here should be regarded as a guide. It might be necessary to make a few slight changes to the order when building your particular PC. Here things will only be considered in a superficial fashion. Detailed instructions for each step are provided in the next chapter.

It will be necessary to mount the power supply in the case if the two have been obtained as separate entities. Power supplies are not always supplied complete with the four bolts needed to fix them to the rear of the case, but the bits and pieces supplied with the case will probably include something suitable. In general, it is easier to fit the motherboard in the case before the drives have been fitted. With some of the smaller cases it can be essential to fit the motherboard first.

It is likely to be much easier to fit the memory modules, processor, heatsink, and fan with the motherboard out of the case. Most modern cases provide good access to the motherboard, but totally unrestricted access with the motherboard outside the case is still preferable. This preassembly should therefore be undertaken before the motherboard is

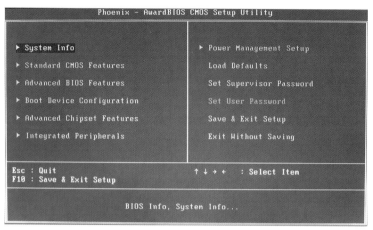

*Fig.1.12  The initial page of a BIOS Setup program*

installed in the case. The mountings for the motherboard should be included with the case, and they are designed to hold any exposed connections on the underside of the board well clear of the case's metal chassis.

The next step is to fit the drives into their bays. The necessary fixing screws are usually supplied with the retail boxed versions of drives, but are unlikely to be included with OEM versions. Suitable fixing screws should be included with the case, so it does not really matter too much if they are not included with the drives. If the case is not already equipped with a cooling fan, fit one at this stage. PC cooling fans are normally supplied with the four rather stubby fixing bolts needed to fit them to the case. A modern PC case usually has provision for several cooling fans of various sizes, so there should be no difficulty in finding a suitable place for it.

With the mechanical side of construction completed, it is then time to start connecting everything together. The order in which the connections are made probably does not matter too much, but try to work in a reasonably methodical manner so that nothing is overlooked. I generally connect the drives to the motherboard first, and then connect the power supply to the motherboard and each of the drives. The fan for the processor should be connected to the motherboard as part of the motherboard's preassembly stage, but the fan for the case can be connected at this point, together with any other miscellaneous

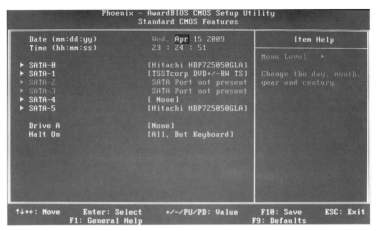

Fig.1.13  The BIOS Setup program has found all the installed disc
         drives

connections to the motherboard such as the on/off switch, power LED,
and any connections to the USB and audio ports on the motherboard.

Assembly of the base unit is complete unless some expansion cards are
required. If a video card or any other cards are needed to complete the
PC, they should be installed at this stage. It is best to leave them until
assembly is otherwise complete, since they can otherwise get in the way
and make it difficult to install the cabling. As a final touch you can use
cable ties to tidy the "rat's nest" of cables and make the interior of the PC
look a bit neater. As a minimum, any cable that is in danger of getting
into the blades of a cooling fan should be secured a safe distance away
from the fan.

With the base unit finished it is time to connect the keyboard and mouse,
connect the PC to the mains supply, and after a final check to ensure
that everything is properly in place, switch on. Of course, at this stage
the computer will not work properly, since there is no operating system
installed on the hard disc. It should go through the POST procedure,
but it will stall with an error message when it tries to boot from the hard
disc drive. Rather than letting this happen, divert the computer into the
BIOS Setup program (Figure 1.12) and make sure that everything is set
correctly. In particular, check that the disc drives have been found and
identified correctly (Figure 1.13).

Then place the installation DVD for the operating system in the DVD
drive, exit the BIOS Setup program and boot into the installation disc.

The facilities provided by this disc enable the hard disc drive to be partitioned and formatted, and then the operating system can be installed using a process that is largely automatic. The computer will boot into the operating system once installation has been completed, and you then have a working PC that is ready for your application programs and data to be installed on the hard disc drive.

At least, in theory the computer is fully working and it is just a matter of installing the required software and your data files. In practice it is a virtual certainty that some of the driver programs installed as part of the Windows installation will be simple generic types that work, but only in a limited fashion. The driver software for some items of hardware will probably be completely absent at this stage. In order to rectify the situation it is necessary to install the driver software that is supplied with the motherboard and some of the other items of hardware.

It is likely that there will be a number of updates available for Windows, and these should be downloaded and installed prior to using the computer in earnest. There might also be some updated driver software available on the Internet, but it is not essential to use the latest drivers unless there are issues with the existing ones. All this additional installation and updating can actually take longer than building the PC and installing the operating system! Anyway, with the proper driver software installed and Windows brought up to date, the application programs and data files can be installed. The computer is then finally ready for use.

# Assembly

## Demo PC

In the previous chapter the basics that you need to understand before getting started were covered, and it is now time to move on to a more detailed look at PC assembly.  The PC I built to provide a basis of this chapter has a fairly modest specification, but it offers a reasonably high level of performance.  It is certainly capable of running the vast majority of modern application programs, and running them well.  These are the main components that were used in the demonstration PC.

- Gigabyte GA-EG41MF-S2H motherboard

- Intel Pentium Dual Core E5400 processor, 2.7GHz

- Heatsink and fan for the processor

- 2GB RAM (two 1GB DDR2-800 memory modules)

- Two Hitachi 160GB SATA hard disc drives

- DVD read/write drive (SATA)

- DVD read/write drive (parallel IDE)

- Flash card reader for various types of card

- MIDI tower case with 450 watt PSU

- 22-inch widescreen LCD monitor

- USB keyboard and mouse

The two hard disc drives were removed from the PC that the new one would replace, and they are much more recent that the rest of the old

*Fig.2.1 The case for the demonstration PC*

PC. Although SATA rather than SATA2 drives, they have a reasonably high capacity and performance. They were certainly far too good to discard, and proved to be more than adequate in the new PC. The DVD drive with the parallel IDE interface is not strictly necessary, since there is also a modern SATA DVD drive. It was mainly included to provide an example of how a parallel IDE interface is used. I use Flash memory cards a great deal when using digital cameras, and when transferring data from one computer to another. A built-in Flash card reader was therefore essential. The same cannot be said for a floppy disc drive, and a drive of this type is not included. However, fitting a floppy disc drive is covered in this chapter.

The USB keyboard and mouse were supplied with another PC, but were never actually used with it. Eventually I removed these and returned to my faithful PS/2 keyboard and USB mouse from the old computer. The old PC had a working 19-inch CRT monitor that no longer produced totally sharp results and was expensive to run. If you do a lot of computing it makes sense to replace a CRT monitor with a modern LCD type even if the old monitor is working well. The lower running costs of an LCD monitor mean that it will probably pay for itself before too long. In this case I obtained a low-cost 22-inch widescreen LCD monitor that, after a little adjustment, provided excellent picture quality.

*Fig.2.2  The left side of the case gives access to the interior*

The case is a low-cost type that came complete with the 450 watt power supply unit. It is a small midi tower, or possibly a large mini tower, but either way it was more than adequate to accommodate the motherboard and five drives. The power supply proved to be quite noisy and to have a slightly inadequate power rating, so it was eventually replaced with a "silent" 650 watt type.

The processor was selected on the basis that it would provide good performance and the price was right. Being a boxed retail version, it came complete with a suitable heatsink and fan. As the ultimate in sound and graphics capability were not considered to be essential features for the new PC, I opted for a motherboard having integrated sound and graphics. The Gigabyte board eventually selected is compatible with processors that use 45nm technology, which is just as well since the processor I chose is of this type!

*Fig.2.3  The right side of the case provides access to one side of the drive cages, but little else*

This motherboard can use single memory modules, but in order to obtain optimum performance it is necessary to make use of the board's dual channel capability. This requires the memory modules to be used in pairs, so the 2 gigabytes of memory is provided by a pair of 1 gigabyte modules. DDR2 modules are used because this is the only type supported by the motherboard.

## Preliminaries

The first task when assembling a PC is to get the case ready for assembly to begin. Unless you obtain one of the more exotic cases there should be no difficulty in opening the case. Removing four or six screws at the rear of the case should release the two side panels of a tower case, or the top and bottom panels of a desktop type. Look carefully to see which screws actually hold the outer casing in position, or you will probably find that you have removed the power supply instead!

The demonstration PC that forms the basis of this chapter has a small tower case (Figure 2.1). The assembly notes will therefore be correct for a case of this type, or any tower type. A tower case is basically just a desktop type used on its side, so the assembly notes apply equally to a desktop type provided you allow for this factor. Figure 2.2 shows the left-hand side of the case, and this is the side that provides access to the interior of the case. This is where the drives, motherboard, and everything else are fitted into the case. Access to the other side of the case (Figure 2.3) will probably be needed when bolting the drives in place, but is unlikely to be necessary apart from this. Figure 2.4 shows the rear of the case, with the power supply fitted

*Fig.2.4  The rear of the case*

at the top, and the blanking plates for the expansion card slots at the bottom.

Inside the case there should be various accessories. A mains lead will probably be included if the case has a power supply already fitted. If not, the mains lead is a standard item that can be obtained cheaply from any computer or electrical store. The end that connects to the computer normally has a standard IEC plug, as used for most mains powered gadgets these days. There will also be various items of hardware such as screws (Figure 2.5), and there might also be two or three metal plates with various holes stamped in them (Figure 2.6). These fit on the rear of the case and accommodate various port configurations.

There are now so many different ATX port arrangements that many case manufacturers do not supply alternative plates. Instead, they leave it to the motherboard manufacturer to supply a plate having the appropriate layout. It is therefore the plate supplied with the motherboard that you

*Fig.2.5 The hardware supplied with the case*

clip into place at the rear of the case. Figure 2.7 shows the ports on the rear of the motherboard used in the demonstration PC, and Figure 2.8 shows the matching plate in place on the finished PC. The plate might not clip into place very securely, but this does not matter too much as it is firmly pinned in place when the motherboard is fitted in the case.

## Stand-offs

The next task is to install the stand-offs on which the motherboard will be mounted. It is possible that these will be built into the chassis, or that

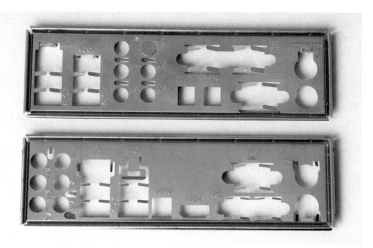

*Fig.2.6 Some metal plates for the port cluster might be included*

*Fig.2.7  The ports of the motherboard used in the demonstration PC*

they will already be fitted to the chassis.  This is unlikely though, and the first part of the assembly process is to fit the stand-offs to the chassis.  If you look at the mounting holes in the motherboard and those in the chassis you will find that there are many more in the chassis.  This is simply because the case is normally designed to take various types of motherboard, large and small, old and new.  Some of the holes in the chassis probably have no relevance to any modern motherboards, and others will probably not be relevant to the particular board you are using.

The only sure way of telling which holes in the chassis should be fitted with stand-offs is to place the motherboard in position inside the case. Once the motherboard is inside the case it can be moved around until all the holes in the board match up with holes in the case.  Make a careful note of which holes in the case should be fitted with stand-offs, making a quick sketch if necessary.

*Fig.2.8  Here the plate supplied with the motherboard is in place on the completed PC*

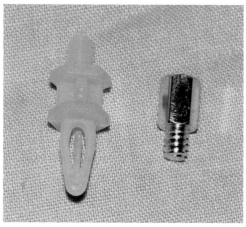

It is possible that there will be some holes in the motherboard that have no counterparts in the case. This was quite normal with the old AT motherboards, but it is less likely to occur with the modern ATX variety. The extra holes can simply be left unused, and provided there are at least half a dozen mounting points spread well across the board it should be held in

*Fig.2.9  Two types of stand-off*

place adequately. Make sure that the board is well supported near the expansion slots, memory modules and the processor. A fair amount of pressure can be placed on the motherboards when an expansion card is fitted. The same is true when the PC is given a memory upgrade or the processor requires a replacement heatsink and fan.

A check through odds and ends of hardware supplied with the board might throw up a few plastic stand-offs. Figure 2.9 shows the normal metal type (right) and the plastic variety (left). The plastic type simply pushes into place in the chassis and the motherboard. They do not provide an electrical connection to the chassis, and do not fix the board in place reliably on their own. Therefore, it is all right to use a mixture of metal and plastic stand-offs, but there should always be at least four or five metal types so that the board is in electrical contact with the chassis and fixed firmly in place.

The odds and ends supplied with the case or the motherboard might include some stand-offs that can be fitted into the underside of the motherboard, but have no provision for fixing to the chassis. These stand-offs are simply pushed into a mounting hole on the underside of the motherboard, and they can be used in any holes that have no counterparts in the case. Motherboards sometimes have extra mounting holes around the processor and (or) memory modules, but as they are non-standard in nature there will be no matching holes in the case. The idea is to provide extra support in areas of the board where pressure might be applied, such as when fitting a processor or memory upgrade.

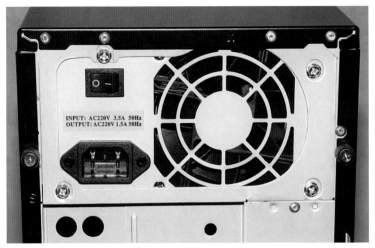

*Fig.2.10  The power supply is fixed to the rear panel by four screws*

Some cases have stand-offs that are non-standard in nature. For instance, I have used cases where the stand-offs are in the form of simple spring clips that fit into square holes in the chassis. If you look at the odds and ends supplied with the case, and then look at the case and chassis, it will not usually be too difficult to figure out how everything fits together. Unfortunately, a PC case is hardly ever supplied with any form of instruction manual or leaflet, although you might find a few helpful illustrations on the box!

## Power supply (PSU)

If the power supply is not already installed in the case, this would probably be a good time to fit it in place. The power supply will probably hinder access to the motherboard and drives, so leaving it until a little later in the assembly process does have its advantages. However, with a modern case it is positioned right at the top of the case where it is not a major hindrance. Anyway, the power supply is fixed to the rear panel of the case using four screws (Figure 2.10) that are the larger type normally used with PCs.

There is sometimes provision for fixing the power supply to the top panel of the case, which prevents the front of the unit drooping slightly. However, this type of thing can only be implemented if the power supply and the

*Fig.2.11 The blanking plates for the expansion slots*

case are fully compatible in this respect. Normally you just have to rely on the four screws to hold it in place. This is less than ideal, but as modern PC power supplies seem to be relatively light it is not something that is likely to become a cause for concern.

## Blanking plates

If the PC will include one or more expansion cards, this would be a good time to remove the corresponding blanking plates at the rear of the computer. This can be left until later, but with some types of plate it is much easier to remove them while the case is empty and access is unrestricted. With the more upmarket cases the blanking plates are each held in place by a single bolt. In fact they are held in place in exactly the same manner as the rear plates on expansion cards. Some cases have blanking plates that can be removed by simply unclipping them.  They can usually be clipped back into place again if the expansion card is removed at some later date.

The most common method is to have so-called "knockout" plates.  With this method the plates are largely cut from the rest of the case, and are only held in place by two or three thin pieces of metal (Figure 2.11).  This approach to things is used a great deal with budget computer cases, and it is a simple way of having optional cut-outs.  Removing an unwanted panel is not difficult, and it is just a matter of pressing it with your finger to break one side free from the case.  Then the panel is waggled backwards and forwards a few times until the fingers of metal securing it to the case fatigue and break.

There may be some rough edges produced where the metal fatigues and breaks.  It is tempting to use a miniature file to rectify this, but filing or cutting a PC case using a saw is not something to be recommended.  The problem is simply that the small metal fragments produced are difficult to thoroughly clean from the case, and they are also good at producing short-circuits if they get onto any of the circuit boards.  If there are any dangerously sharp edges they must be removed, but otherwise do not bother.  If you do have to file away any sharp edges try to thoroughly clean away any swarf.  A damp rag does the job quite well, but the sticky side of adhesive tape or some Bostik Blu-Tack are probably the most effective ways of mopping up the swarf.

Most motherboards have several PCI expansion slots, and some people seem to be under the impression that they have to be used in a particular order.  This is not the case though, and where (say) two PCI expansions are to be fitted, they do not have to be used in PCI slots 1 and 2.  They will work just as well in slots 3 and 4, slots 2 and 7, or any other two slots.  Installing the cards is generally easier if they are well spaced apart rather than clumped together, but apart from this it does not matter which ones are used.

## Configuration

Assembly now switches to the preassembly of the motherboard.  In days gone by it was necessary to start by configuring various switches and (or) jumper contacts on the motherboard.  Most modern motherboards are of the so-called "jumperless" variety, and have nothing to set up prior to installation in the case.  The configuration is handled entirely using the BIOS Setup program, and the configuration data is stored in CMOS memory that retains its contents even when the computer is switched off.

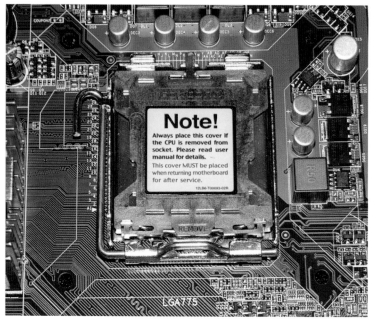

Fig.2.12  The socket for the processor is protected by a plastic cover

Fig.2.13  Here the socket has been opened

*Fig.2.14  The connections on the underside of the processor*

It is best not to jump to conclusions though, and the motherboard's instruction manual should be checked for details of any setting up that might be required. In most cases there is actually one jumper fitted on the motherboard, but this is only needed if it should become necessary to clear the contents of the CMOS memory and start from scratch. The normal procedure is to switch off the computer using the mains on/off switch on the power supply or the mains outlet, remove the jumper, wait a few seconds, and then fit the jumper again. Clearing the CMOS memory is only likely to become necessary if you use the password feature in the BIOS Setup program and then forget the password, making it impossible to start booting the computer into the operating system!

## Fitting the processor

The conventional arrangement is for the processor to have hundreds of pins on the underside, which fit into a socket on the motherboard. There is a lever beside the socket on the motherboard, and this lever is raised in order to unlock the socket. The processor can then be dropped into

*Fig.2.15  The top side of the processor, which is still in its anti-static packing*

place in the socket, and the lever is then lowered in order to lock the processor in place.  Things are a bit different with the Intel Socket 775 processor used in this PC.  The socket on the motherboard actually has hundreds of pins, and what would conventionally be considered the socket is actually on the underside of the processor.  This is not really of any practical consequence, since fitting the processor is much the same either way.  Fitting a processor into an Intel 775 socket is slightly more involved than using other types of processor though.

Another departure from the normal scheme of things is that the "socket" on the motherboard has a protective cover for the pins (Figure 2.12). This is hinged and can be raised when the locking lever is raised (Figure 2.13).  The plastic part of the cover must be removed, and this is simply a matter of carefully pressing it out of place.

Next the processor is fitted in place.  Figure 2.14 shows the underside of the processor, which is still in its transparent anti-static packing.  Normally there would be rows of pins here, but as explained previously, with a Socket 775 processor you have the socket on the processor and the

*Fig.2.16  The plastic cover has been removed and the processor is in place, but the socket is still open*

pins on the motherboard.  The top side of the processor is shown in Figure 2.15.  Although the standard anti-static handling precautions will be taken when dealing with the processor, it is still advisable to avoid touching the contacts on the underside of this component whenever handling it.

The motherboard is fitted with a ZIF (zero insertion force) socket, so the processor should simply drop into place provided it has the correct orientation.  Never try to force a processor into its socket as this is likely to seriously damage the processor, the motherboard, or both.  If it does not simply drop into place there is something wrong, such as the socket's release lever not being fully raised or the processor having the wrong orientation.

There are markers on the processor and the motherboard that should make it easy to get the processor the right way round first time. Unfortunately, in practice there can be a bewildering assortment of marks, or they can be absent.  Typically there is a small triangular mark in one corner of the processor, and a similar mark on the corresponding corner of the socket on the motherboard.  In this example the (more or less) triangular mark on one corner of the processor is easy enough to spot, but the corresponding mark on the motherboard is easier to miss than it is to find.  If necessary, you can resort to trial and error to find the correct orientation, but it has to be emphasised again that the processor should

not be forced into place. Once everything is just right it will simply drop into place. If it does not drop into place, everything is not all right.

Figures 2.16 and 2.17 show two views of the processor correctly seated in its socket. It must be locked in place, and to do this it is just a matter lowering the remaining part of the cover, and then the lever is used to lock

*Fig.2.17 Another view of the processor in place*

*Fig.2.18 The processor has been locked in place*

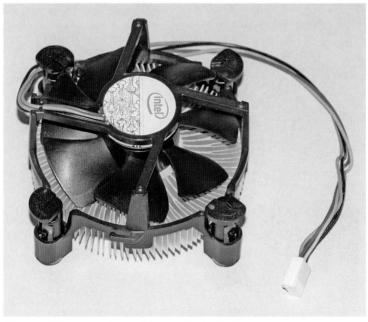

*Fig.2.19 The fan and heatsink supplied with the processor*

the processor and cover in place (Figure 2.18). Check that everything is properly locked in place, and it is then time to fit the heatsink and fan onto the processor.

## Heatsink and fan

Processor heatsinks have tended to become larger and more elaborate over the years, and the fans tend to be much larger than they used to be. The top and underside of the heatsink and fan supplied with the processor are shown in Figure 2.19 and 2.20 respectively. By current standards it is a fairly modest example of a heatsink and fan.

The underside of the heatsink must be covered with some silicone grease, or something of that ilk, to provide a good thermal contact between the heatsink and the top of the processor. Thermal compounds are available from the large suppliers of computer parts, but in most cases it is not necessary to buy any. The heatsink normally has a pad of thermal

*Fig.2.20  The underside of the heatsink*

compound already in place on the underside, and in Figure 2.20 there are three pads of this material in the centre of the heatsink. It is only necessary to buy some thermal compound if the heatsink is not supplied complete with any, or it is but the pad of compound becomes damaged to the point where it might not fulfil its function.

In use the compound tends to spread out when the heatsink is pressed down onto the top of the processor, and it spreads still further when the processor gets hot and the compound softens. The thermal compound fills every minute nook and granny, avoiding minuscule air gaps and ensuring a good thermal contact. Modern processors consume relatively large amounts of power, especially when they are performing some intensive processing. Without an efficient heatsink and fan, and a good thermal contact between the processor and the heatsink, there is a danger of the processor overheating. Modern motherboards usually have

*Fig.2.21  The heatsink and fan installed on the motherboard*

sophisticated temperature sensors that will detect a dangerously high processor temperature and shut down the PC before any damage occurs. However, it is advisable not to put this type of thing to the test!

In Figure 2.20 it is possible to see a white plastic fastener at the end of each of the four "legs". There are four holes in the motherboard to take these fasteners, and these can be seen in Figure 2.17. They are just simple holes drilled in the motherboard, and the business part of the fixing system is on the heatsink. In order to fit the heatsink in place it is just a matter of aligning the four fasteners with the holes in the motherboard, and then pressing down on each of the four "legs" to fit the fasteners into place. A "click" should be heard as each one locks into place. The method usually recommended is to press two diagonally opposite "legs" into place simultaneously, but this can be a bit difficult with some heatsinks. With this type of thing you often have to "play it by ear" and use a little common sense.

Once all four fastenings have been fitted it is advisable to pull on the heatsink to check that it is not loose at one corner. If one of the fasteners

*Fig.2.22  This is a conventional socket for an AMD processor*

fails to lock in place, check its alignment and try again.  Figure 2.21 shows the heatsink and fan correctly locked in place on a motherboard.  Note that once in place it is not possible to remove the heatsink simply by pulling it free.  There is usually a slot for a screwdriver at the top of each "leg", and about a quarter of a turn in a counter-clockwise direction should free each one so that the heatsink can be easily lifted from the motherboard.

There are currently several different methods of fixing heatsinks in place, and the manufacturers seem to come up with a steady flow of new types.  Retail boxed processors are supplied with an instruction leaflet that explains how the heatsink is fitted in place, so if in doubt you can always refer to this.  A heatsink obtained separately from the processor should also be supplied complete with fixing instructions, but some lack worthwhile fitting instructions.  Clearly it is essential to be very careful when buying a processor and heatsink separately, as it would be very easy to end up with a heatsink that did not match the fixing method used by the motherboard.  Buying a retail boxed processor, complete with heatsink and fan, is a much safer option, and should not be significantly more expensive.

*Fig.2.23  Here an AMD processor has been locked into its socket*

## Other processors

The method used to fit most processors into their sockets is simpler than the one used to fit a processor to a Socket 775 motherboard. With most processors it is just a matter of lifting the lever to unlock the ZIF socket, dropping the processor into place, and then lowering the lever again in order to lock the processor in the socket. Figure 2.22 shows an AMD Socket 939 motherboard with the socket empty and the socket unlocked. Figure 2.23 shows the same board with a processor locked in place.

## Fan power

The cooling fan will require a 12-volt supply, and there are two normal ways of obtaining power for a fan. In the past the most common method was to obtain power from one of the 5.25-in. disc drive supply outputs of the power supply unit. There will not always be a spare output of this type, but some PC cooling fans are fitted with a lead that has two

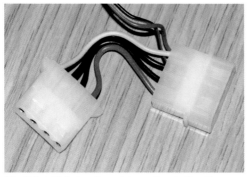

*Fig.2.24  This lead enables a fan to "tap" power from a 5.25-inch IDE drive*

connectors (Figure 2.24). One of these connects to the output of the power supply and other connects to a 5.25-in. drive. This enables a single output of the power supply to provide power to both the cooling fan and one of the drives. If you use this method of powering the fan it is obviously not connected to the power supply until the motherboard has been finally installed in the case.

The alternative method, and by far the most common one these days for a processor fan, is to power the fan from the motherboard. Modern motherboards have a small three-pin connector (Figure 2.25) that can supply 12 volts to the cooling fan, and practically all processor cooling fans are now fitted with this type of connector. The fans fitted to the heatsinks for Intel processors sometimes have a four-way connector, and the motherboard might have a matching four-pin type. The four-way connectors used on the fans are compatible with three-pin motherboard connectors, so there should be no great problem if the motherboard only has a three-pin type. There is no need to worry about getting fan connectors fitted the right way round, because they will only fit with the correct orientation. If the fan is powered in this way it should be connected to the motherboard as soon as it has been fitted on the processor.

On the face of it, a two-way connector is adequate to provide power to a fan. The third connection is used to send a signal from the fan to the motherboard so that the BIOS or an application program can monitor the speed of the fan. The general idea is for a warning to be given if the speed of the fan is too low or no fan is detected. In fact the BIOS might prevent the computer from starting if no fan is detected.

Modern motherboards often have more than one power supply output for a fan. If this should be the case the motherboard's instruction manual should indicate which output to use for the processor's fan. It is important to use this one for the processor's fan, and it is definitely not a good idea to leave it unused. The motherboards will sense that there is not an operating fan connected on the processor fan's output, which could cause warning alarms to sound or prevent the PC starting. The same problem can arise if the fan is powered from a 5.25-inch drive supply. The safest option is to power the fan from the correct output on the motherboard.

*Fig.2.25  A 3-pin power output for a fan*

Powering the case cooling fan from a 5.25-inch drive power connector is less problematic, but the BIOS usually has a facility for monitoring this fan as well. This facility can only work if the fan is powered from the motherboard, and the fan has the third connection needed by the monitoring feature. Where possible, it best to power both fans from the motherboard, and to also have the BIOS set up to monitor both of them.

## Fitting memories

The next stage is to install the memory on the motherboard. Modern motherboards use some form of DIMM (dual in-line memory module). Whether it is the original DDR memory or the latest DDR3 type, the

*Fig.2.26  A DDR2 memory module*

*Fig.2.27  A DDR memory module fitted into its holder but not yet locked in place*

memory will still be in the form of one or more DIMMs.  Fitting DIMMs is very easy, and it is impossible to fit them the wrong way round because the DIMM's circuit board has a polarising "key". This is just an off-centre notch cut in the circuit board that matches a bar in the DIMM socket. Figure 2.26 shows a DDR DIMM, which is the most commonly used type at present.  The key is apparently in a slightly different position depending on the supply voltage of the module and the type of RAM fitted, and there are two keys in some DIMMs.  These differences should make it impossible to fit a DIMM of the wrong type.

Because one notch and bar are well off-centre it is easy to determine which way around the module should go. The module simply drops into place vertically and as it is pressed down into position the plastic lever at each end of the socket should start to close up.  Pressing both levers into a fully vertical position should securely lock the module in place, if the levers do not snap into position of their own accord.  Make sure the levers are pulled fully outwards before you try to fit the DIMM.  Figures

*Fig.2.28  The two "arms" have locked the memory module in place*

*Fig.2.29  The DVD is behind this flap in the front panel*

2.27 and 2.28 respectively show a DIMM that is ready to be pushed down into place, and one that is locked in place. To remove a DIMM, simply press the two levers outwards as far as they will go. This should unlock the memory module so that it can be lifted free of the socket.

Once the memory modules have been fitted the motherboard is installed in the case. This should be perfectly straightforward provided the case has been prepared correctly, and the appropriate stand-offs are in position on the chassis. Leave the mounting screws slightly loose until they are all in position. You might otherwise find that the board has been fixed slightly out of position by the first one or two fixing bolts, making it impossible to fit the others in place.

## Drives

With all the motherboard's fixings in place and properly tightened it is time to progress to the next step, which is to install the drives in the drive bays. There are plastic covers over the external drive bays, and these must be removed at the positions where drives are to be fitted. These are easily pushed out from the rear, but there will probably be a slight snag here in the form of a metal plate behind each plastic cover. These

plates are partially cut from the case, and must be removed from any bays where externally accessible drives will be fitted. They can usually be left in place where other drives, such as the hard drive or drives, will be fitted.

*Fig.2.30  The tray has pushed the flap down and out of the way*

They are removed in the same way as other blanking plates in the case. Remove the plastic cover first. There are usually a couple of holes in the metal plate so that you can push out the plastic cover from the rear by poking a screwdriver through one of these holes. With a bit of pushing and shoving it should be possible to turn the plate through about 30 degrees or so, although it can take a while to get the blanking plate completely free. You can then get hold of one edge, and with a bit of waggling the plate should soon break away from the case.

*Fig.2.31  Two bolts on each side of a drive are sufficient to fix it reliably*

With the plate and plastic cover removed the bay is ready for the drive to be fitted. Note that with some of the more expensive cases the metal plates are held in place by two or four screws, so check for these before trying to break the plates free! It is increasingly common for cases to have a hinged cover at the front of one or more of the externally accessible 5.25-inch drive bays.

*Fig.2.32 The upper side of a hard disc drive is usually enclosed*

The idea is that you push the button on the cover, this presses the button on the front of the drive, and the drive's tray then pops out, pushing the hinged cover downwards (Figures 2.29 and 2.30). This type of thing is fine if it works with total reliability, but it is otherwise better to remove the hinged cover and fit the drive normally. It will only work at all if the drive is mounted as far forward as possible so that pressing the button on the cover activates the button on the front of the drive.

It is likely that there will be more drive bays than drives, leaving some of the bays unused. It does not really matter too much which bays you leave unused, but where possible it is probably better to arrange things so that there is an unused bay between drives. Spacing out the drives often makes installation slightly less fiddly, and it can also make them easier to use. Another factor is that many modern drives get quite hot when they have been in use for a while. Spacing them out as much as possible makes it easier for the air to circulate and should help to keep the drives cool.

With modern cases there should be no difficulty in fitting the drives since they mostly slot direct into the bays. Suitable fixing screws should be

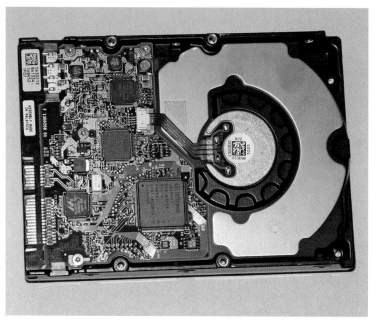

*Fig.2.33  The underside of a hard disc drive is usually open, revealing
         a circuit board and part of the mechanism*

supplied with the case, and will probably be included with some of the
drives as well.  It is best to use only the screws supplied with the drive or
case, as they are suitably short.  Screws even slightly longer might
penetrate too far into the drive and cause severe damage.  Where
appropriate, the fixing screws that are supplied with a drive should always
be used, since they will presumably be a perfect fit for the drive.  Some
of the screws supplied with the case should do the job perfectly well
though.

There are usually four mounting holes in each side of 5.25-inch drives
but it is only necessary to use two fixing screws in each side (Figure
2.31).  Initially leave the screws slightly loose, and then manoeuvre the
drive precisely into the right position so that its front panel is flush with
the case's front panel.  Then tighten the screws, being careful not to shift
the drive out of position.

Getting the drives the right way up is easy with drives that are accessed
externally, since it is self-evident.  It is not obvious with the hard disc

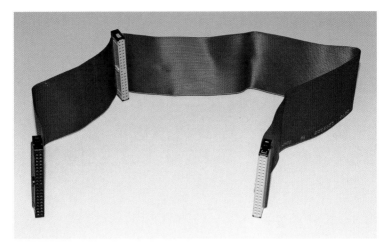

*Fig.2.34  A standard parallel IDE cable for one or two drives*

drive or drives, and this type of drive is unlikely to fit properly unless it is the right way up.  The top side of the drive is normally enclosed, as in Figure 2.32.  The bottom side is normally open with part of the mechanism and a circuit board often visible (Figure 2.33).

## Cabling

It is best to complete the cabling next, prior to installing the expansion cards (which tend to get in the way and make it difficult to fit the cables). The motherboard should be supplied complete with a basic set of connecting cables.  For a budget ATX board this will probably just be a data cable for the floppy disc drive, another one for parallel IDE drives, and one or two for SATA or SATA2 drives.

The parallel IDE cable (Figure 2.34) will probably support two drives. You might be supplied with the round version of an IDE cable (Figure 2.35).  These are generally a bit easier to use than the flat type, and they are also less of a hindrance to ventilation, but the two types of cable are used in exactly the same way.  These days the floppy cable (Figure 2.36) will probably accommodate a single drive.  This is reasonable, given that few modern PCs have even one drive, let alone two of them.  The SATA data cables (Figure 2.37) will each support a single drive, as does each SATA port on the motherboard.

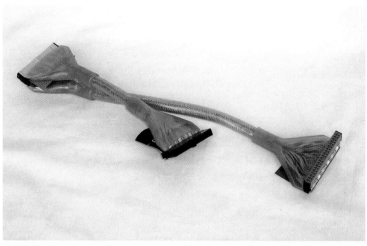

*Fig.2.35  The "round" version of an IDE data cable has its advantages*

With a modern PC it is quite likely that there will only be one IDE port on the motherboard, and it is by no means certain that even a single IDE port will be needed.  Modern hard disc drives and CD/DVD drives have a SATA or SATA2 interface, which leaves the IDE port unused unless you wish to use an old drive in the new PC.  The motherboard used in the demonstration PC has a single IDE port, which is the green coloured one in Figure 2.38.  The port on the rear of an IDE drive is essentially the same as the one on the motherboard, and all the connectors on an IDE cable are of the same type.

*Fig.2.36  A floppy disc data cable, complete with "twist" near the left end*

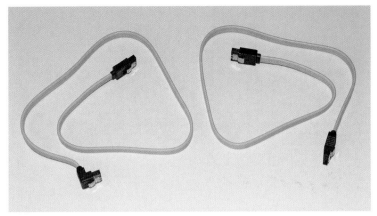

*Fig.2.37  Two SATA data cables*

In theory the IDE connectors are polarised and can only be fitted the right way round.  In practice some of the connectors, especially the ones on cheaper motherboards, are rather basic and are not properly polarised. The plugs on the motherboards and drives should each have a cut-out in the plastic surround, and this should match up with a protrusion on each plug.  The polarising keys are clearly visible along the bottom edge

*Fig.2.38  The green connector is a parallel IDE port*

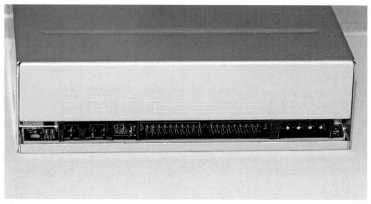

*Fig.2.39  The rear of a parallel IDE DVD drive*

of the IDE connector in Figure 2.38. These days there is usually a missing pin on the motherboard and drive connectors. The absent pin is near the middle of the top row in Figure 2.38, or perhaps that should be it is not present near the middle of the top row. The connectors on the IDE lead have the corresponding hole filled in, making it impossible to fit the lead connectors the wrong way round. This is the more reliable of the two methods of polarising the connectors.

The two devices on an IDE port are called the "master" and "slave" devices. It does not matter which drive you connect to which connector on the IDE cable. Jumpers on the device itself control the role of an IDE device. If there is only one device on an IDE port it is normally set up as the master, but the system should work just as well if it is set as the slave device. The jumper is used to bridge the two "S" or "SL" terminals if it is to be the slave device or the

*Fig.2.40  A close-up view of the jumper connections*

"M" or "MA" terminals if it is to be the "master" drive. In figure 2.39 the jumper terminals are just to the left of the main data connector, and Figure 2.40 shows a close-up view of this part of the drive.

Hard disc drives normally operate using a similar arrangement, but when used as a master device some drives are not quite as straightforward as this. A different jumper configuration can be needed depending on whether or not there is a slave device on that IDE port. The Master setting is then only used if there is a slave device on the same IDE interface as the hard drive. The alternative setting, which will be called something like the Sole setting, is used if the hard disc is the only drive on that IDE interface.

You should always check the instruction manuals of IDE drives to see if there are any unusual aspects to the configuration, and then proceed accordingly. Retail boxed drives are usually supplied with a detailed instruction manual, but the OEM units are usually "bare" drives. Instruction manuals for hard disc drives are usually available from the manufacturer's web site. The vast majority of modern drives have a configuration diagram or chart marked on the actual drive. Altering the jumper settings on some drives is fiddly and awkward, but it is generally a bit easier if it is done prior to fitting the drives in the case.

## Floppy cable

Rather than using jumpers to set one floppy drive as drive A and the other as drive B, a twist in part of a twin floppy cable sets the drive designations. The twist can be seen near the left end of the cable in Figure 2.36. With a modern PC it is unlikely that more than one floppy drive will be fitted. The connector near the twist then connects to the single floppy drive and the other end connects to the floppy connector on the motherboard (the black connector in Figure 2.41). This drive will be designated drive A by the operating system. If there is a connector near the middle of the cable, it is for a second drive, which will be designated as drive B by the operating system. The type of connector used on floppy cables is a smaller version of the type used for parallel IDE devices (34 terminals instead of 40), and the same method of polarisation is used.

## Serial ATA (SATA)

Drive configuration with Serial ATA drives is very straightforward. They do not require any! Serial ATA operates on the basis of having an

*Fig.2.41 The black connector is the port for floppy disc drives*

individual interface for each drive.  Modern motherboards usually have at least four Serial ATA ports (Figure 2.42), but just one IDE type.  Four ports are sufficient to accommodate something like two hard disc drives and two DVD types, which is adequate for most users, rendering IDE ports unnecessary unless you have an old drive of this type that you wish to use in the computer.

The connectors used for SATA drives are properly polarised and easy to fit.  These cables do not have a "computer" end and a "drive" end, and can be used either way round.  It does not seem to matter which port you use for each drive, but it is probably best to be logical about things and use port 1 for the boot drive. If there is a second hard disc drive, connect this to port 2. The DVD drive that will be used to install the operating system should be connected to port 3, or port 2 if only one hard disc drive is

*Fig.2.42  A modern motherboard usually has at least four SATA2 ports*

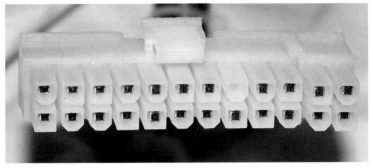

*Fig.2.43  A 24-way power connector.  The block of four terminals at the right end can be removed to leave a 20-way type*

fitted.  Any other CD/DVD drives are simply connected to the lowest number ports that are available.

## Power supply

The next step is to connect the power supply to the motherboard and the disc drives.  The main power connector will probably be a 24-way type.  If you refer back to Figure 2.38, the white connector at the bottom is the motherboard version of a 24-way power connector.  Figure 2.43 shows the corresponding connector of the power supply, and in Figure 2.44 the power supply's connector has been fitted to the motherboard.

*Fig.2.44  A 24-way power lead connected to the motherboard*

*Fig.2.45  The white connector is a 20-way power  type*

The connectors are polarised and cannot be fitted the wrong way round. This is also a locking connector system, so the little lever on the plug must be pressed before trying to pull it free of the socket on the motherboard. Make sure that the power connector is fully pushed down into place. It will not connect to the motherboard properly unless it fully in position and locked in place.

*Fig.2.46  There is often an additional 4-way power lead*

There is a slight complication with the main power

*Fig.2.47  A 4-way power connector on a motherboard*

connector, which is that some motherboards and supplies have the old 20-way type instead of the modern 24-pin variety. Figure 2.45 shows the motherboard version of a 20-way power connector (the white connector near the top). The 24-way plug on a power supply lead cannot be connected to a 20-way socket on a motherboard, but with many supplies it is possible to detach part of the connector, leaving a 20-way type. Although most motherboards have a 24-way power connector, many of them will quite happily accommodate and use a 20-way power plug. If you intend to try this, check the instruction manual for

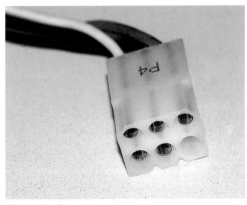

*Fig.2.48  Sometimes an extra power connector is used, such as this 6-way type*

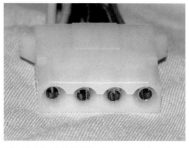

*Fig.2.49  A 5.25-inch power lead*

the motherboard to see if it is acceptable with the particular board you are using.

The motherboard will usually have one or two additional power connectors to deal with. The most common of these is a 4-way type (Figures 2.46 and 2.47), which is a sort of miniature version of the main power connector that locks into place in the same way. The PCI Express power connectors are used to a far lesser degree. The 6-way version of a PCI Express power connector is shown in Figure 2.48, and it is again a sort of miniature version of the main power connector, that locks into place in the same way.

Next the power supply is connected to the drives. Parallel IDE hard disc drives use the power connectors shown in Figure 2.49, as do parallel IDE CD-ROM and DVD drives. Getting this type of connector into place can require a substantial amount of force. It can require even more effort to remove one again. I normally advise people not to use the "hammer and tongs" approach with computer equipment, but you have to be prepared to use a certain amount of brute force with this type of connector. Due to their shape it is impossible to fit these connectors the wrong way round.

*Fig.2.50  The power lead for a 3.5-inch floppy disc drive*

The power lead for a 3.5-inch floppy disc drive is shown in Figure 2.50, and Figure 2.51 shows the rear of a floppy drive. The power port is the small connector on the extreme left-end of the rear panel. Floppy power connectors are polarised and need relatively little force to connect them to the drives. If you find it difficult to fit these plugs into the drives you either have them upside-down, or out of alignment with the connectors in the drive. The concave side of the connector faces downward and

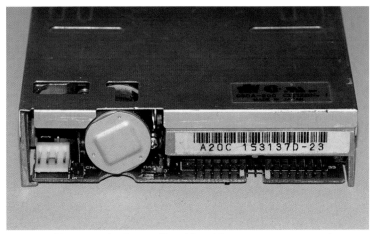

*Fig.2.51  The rear of a floppy disc drive.  The power connector is on the extreme left*

the convex surface faces upwards.  There can be problems with the terminals on the floppy drive's connector getting bent slightly upwards, making it impossible to fit the power connector on the supply lead. Pressing the terminals down slightly should permit the supply to be connected.  Make sure that you get the floppy power connector fitted just right.  Mistakes here can have dire consequences for the power supply and (or) the floppy drive.

## SATA Power

The normal type of power connector for any type of SATA drive is the miniature type shown in Figure 2.52.  SATA drives sometimes have standard 5.25-inch power connectors in addition to their own miniature type, but most only have the miniature power port.

*Fig.2.52  The connector on a SATA power lead*

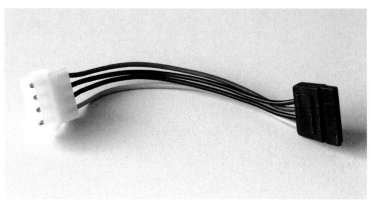

*Fig.2.53  A SATA power adaptor*

Unfortunately, by no means all PC power supplies have sufficient SATA power connectors for even a fairly basic PC that only uses this type of drive. The supply units seem to be designed on the basis that SATA

*Fig.2.54  The connector block for the features provided by the case*

*Fig.2.55  A typical set of leads for the switches, lights, etc., of a case*

hard disc drives and parallel IDE CD-ROM/DVD drives will be used.  Doing things this way is still a possibility, but parallel IDE drives seem to be a dying breed.

Where a drive has a 5.25-inch power port, using it will probably be the best option as it leaves a SATA power connector available for another drive.  In most cases it will be necessary to power at least one serial ATA drive from a 5.25-inch power lead using an adaptor.  The example shown in Figure 2.53 enables one SATA drives to be powered from a 5.25-inch power lead, but there is also a type that provides two SATA power leads.  Another type of adaptor has one SATA input connector and provides two SATA power leads.  Serial ATA power leads are polarised and usually fit into place with a minimum of fuss.

## Connector block

The motherboard will have a connector block that accepts leads from various items on the case (Figure 2.54).  This block is a common cause of confusion for newcomers to PC building because the facilities of the case never seem to perfectly match up with those of the motherboard. A typical set of connectors for an ATX case is shown in Figure 2.55. There may be some features of the case that are not supported by the motherboard, and there will almost certainly be several motherboard features that the case is unable to accommodate.

This is something where you have to take a down-to-earth attitude, and provided a few basic features are implemented on both, which they will be, that is all that is needed to get your new PC operating successfully. These are the functions that you should be able to implement:

### Power LED

This connects to a LED on the front of the case that is on whenever the computer is operating. Note that a LED, unlike an ordinary light bulb, will only work if it is connected with the right polarity. The instruction manual for the motherboard will have a diagram showing the functions of the various pins in the block, and this with have a "+" sign on one of the pins that connects to the power LED. The connectors on the leads that connect to the LEDs, etc., will be marked with their functions, and the connector for the power LED might have its polarity marked. If not, it is usually the white lead that is the "−" connection and the coloured lead that is the "+" one. There is little risk of a LED being damaged if it is connected with the wrong polarity, so you can use trial and error if necessary.

### IDE/SATA activity LED

This is sometimes called the hard disc light, and in days gone by it would probably only switch on when the hard disc was active. However, this light actually switches on when any IDE or SATA device is active. This LED must be connected with the right polarity. Again, trial and error can be used if necessary.

### Reset switch

This is the switch on the front panel that can be used to reset the computer if it hangs up. Its lead can be connected either way round. Some users prefer not to connect this switch, so that it is not possible to accidentally reset the computer. However, without the reset switch the only means of providing a hardware reset is to switch the computer off, wait at least a couple of seconds, and then switch on again.

## Loudspeaker

This is the lead for the computer's internal loudspeaker, which is little used in modern computers. This loudspeaker is normally used to produce one or two beeps at start-up to indicate that all is well or a different set of beeps if there is a fault. It is also used by the temperature sensing and alarm circuits of the BIOS, which can usually be set to produce an alarm if the processor exceeds a certain temperature. The leads on this connector will probably be red and black, but it can actually be connected either way round and it is not polarised. It seems to be quite common for the case to lack a loudspeaker. I suppose it is far from essential, but it is still something I prefer to include. The case for the demonstration PC lacked a loudspeaker so I installed one that was salvaged from a defunct PC.

## Power switch

With an ATX power supply the on/off switching is controlled via a signal from the motherboard. The on/off switch on the front panel connects to the power supply via the motherboard and the supply's main power output lead. Pressing the power switch turns on the computer, pressing it again switches off the computer, and so on. This switch appears to operate like a normal power switch, but note that the computer will be in the off state if the mains supply is removed and then reinstated. Note also, that with a modern PC the on/off switch might do something other than switch off the computer. It will usually set it to a standby mode or do nothing at all. Its "off" function is normally controlled via a power management setting in the operating system. This lead can be connected either way round.

These are some of the functions that might be implemented on the motherboard, but they are non-essential:

## Keylock

It used to be standard practice for PCs to have a key that could be used to operate a special type of switch fitted on the front panel. This switch enabled the keyboard to be switched off, thus preventing anyone from tampering with the PC while you were not looking. This feature was never very popular, and when control of PCs was partially handed over to the mouse it failed to fulfil its intended task anyway. It is probably not worth implementing even if this feature is supported by the case.

*Fig.2.56 A motherboard usually has three types of expansion slot*

### Temperature warning

Because modern PCs contain a lot of components that get quite hot it is now very common for some sort of temperature monitoring and warning feature to be included on motherboards. Exactly what happens when something in the PC starts to get too hot varies from one motherboard to another, but the internal loudspeaker will probably start to "beep", a warning LED might start flashing, or the PC might even switch itself off. If there is an output for a temperature warning LED and the case has a spare LED indicator, I would recommend implementing this feature. Note that the LED will only work if it is connected the right way round. Most facilities of this type have the LED normally switched on, and it flashes when an excessive temperature is detected.

### Suspend switch

This switch can be used to enable and disable the power management function. This is probably something you can live without, which is just as well since few cases have the necessary switch. There is sometimes an output for a LED which operates in conjunction with this feature. With modern motherboards the suspend feature is not usually implemented, but there is often an output for a "suspend" or "message" LED. This is activated when the operating system is placed into the standby mode.

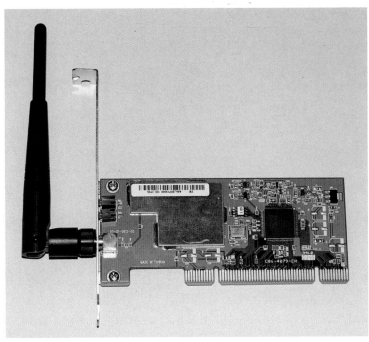

*Fig.2.57 This PCI expansion card is a wi-fi adaptor*

There may well be other functions available, and it is a matter of consulting the motherboard's instruction manual for details of any additional features. However, unless the case has some spare switches and (or) LEDs any "extras" will only be of academic interest. The modern trend is for cases to have a minimum of switches and indicator lights, leaving plenty of space for drives, front panel audio and USB connectors, etc.

## On the cards

By this stage the PC is nearly complete, and the only major task remaining is to fit the various expansion cards. A modern motherboard usually has three types of expansion slot, which are the PCI Express 1X and 16X types, and the PCI variety. In Figure 2.56 the two white slots near the bottom are ordinary PCI slots, the blue one near the middle is the PCI Express 16X type, and the small white slot near the top is the 1X PCI Express slot. The 16X PCI Express slot is for a video card, and the AGP

*Fig.2.58 The locking lever on a 16X PCI Express expansion slot*

type is now obsolete. The PCI and 1X PCI slots are for any expansion cards other than the video variety. Ordinary PCI slots were supposed to be phased out in favour of the 1X PCI Express type, but so far this has not happened. Most expansion cards are still ordinary PCI types, such as the wi-fi card shown in Figure 2.57.

The expansion cards should fit into place without having to push too hard. If a moderate amount of force fails to get one or more of the cards into position it is likely that the motherboard is slightly out of alignment with the case. Try slackening the motherboard's mounting screws slightly, fitting a couple of expansion cards, and then tightening the mounting screws again. It should then be easy to fit any remaining expansion cards, remembering to bolt the metal bracket of each card to the rear of the case.

If it is still difficult to fit one or two of the expansion cards the most likely cause of the problem is the metal bracket at the rear of the offending card or cards. If you look at the rear of the case you will notice that there are receptacles to take the bottom sections of the mounting brackets. With some expansion cards it is necessary to carefully bend the lower section of the mounting bracket backwards so that it engages with the receptacle in the case. Everything should then slot nicely into position.

A suitable video card must be installed if you have not opted for a motherboard that has integrated video. Fitting a 16X PCI Express video card is slightly different to fitting a PCI or 1X PCI Express type. There is a locking lever at the front of the expansion slot, and this lever is clearly visible at the front of the slot in Figure 2.58. It is quite

*Fig.2.59  The audio input for a CD drive*

common for expansion cards to ride up slightly at the front when the mounting bolt is tightened. The connector of a 16X PCI Express card has so many terminals in such a small space that even a small degree of tilt can prevent it from connecting to the motherboard properly. The purpose of the locking mechanism is to ensure that the card cannot ride up slightly at the front.

Fitting a PCI Express video card is actually much the same as installing any other expansion card, but you have to check that the locking mechanism has engaged properly with the card, and that it is holding the card in place securely. Obviously you have to ensure that the card is properly unlocked before trying to remove it, and this simply requires the locking lever to be moved sideways away from the card. It is worth noting that a 16X PCI Express slot will work with 1X PCI Express expansion cards. Therefore, the 16X PCI Express slot could still be useful as a general purpose expansion slot if integrated graphics are being used.

## Audio cable

The PC is now complete apart from any additional cables that have to be connected. At one time it was normal to connect the audio output at the rear of a CD/DVD drive to the audio input of the soundcard or the motherboard. This enables the audio signal from the drive to be played through the computer's sound system. The more normal approach these days is to play audio CDs by reading the digital data and decoding it

*Fig.2.60  The case's front panel audio lead*

using a suitable player, such as the Windows Media Player program.

The audio input is still present on most audio cards, and it is also to be found on motherboards that have integrated audio (Figure 2.59). If you buy a retail-boxed CD/DVD drive and it has an audio output socket, an audio lead will probably be included. It is up to you whether it is connected or omitted. This lead will probably be unnecessary, but there is no harm in including it.

A modern motherboard that has integrated sound will have a full set of audio ins and outs in the main cluster of ports at the rear of the board. Some or all of the audio inputs and outputs will also be available via a

*Fig.2.61  The green connector is for the front panel audio sockets*

secondary connector elsewhere on the motherboard. These days most PC cases have microphone and headphone sockets on the front panel, and they can be connected to the secondary audio connector. The plug on the audio lead in the case will probably look something like the one in Figure 2.60, and the connector on the motherboard is usually like the one shown in Figure 2.61. These connectors are polarised and cannot be connect the wrong way round.

Some cases have individual connectors rather than the standard multi-way type. Fitting each of these to the correct pin is a bit fiddly, but the motherboard's instruction manual should indicate the function of every pin on the secondary audio connector, and the individual

Fig.2.62 The case's front panel USB lead

connectors on the case's audio lead should be marked with their functions. With a bit of effort it can be done.

In a similar vein, there are USB ports in the main cluster at the rear of the motherboard, but there are usually two additional USB connectors elsewhere on the motherboard, with each of these supporting two USB ports. They can be used with the USB sockets that are to be found on the front panels of most PC cases. These days the USB connectors are well standardised, and the type shown in Figure 2.62 is used on the

Fig.2.63 The two yellow connectors are for additional USB ports

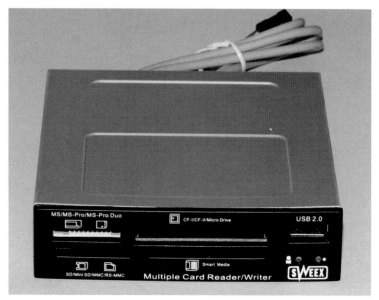

*Fig.2.64 This Flash card reader also provides one USB port*

case's USB lead or leads. The matching type of Figure 2.63 is used on the motherboard. The USB connectors are polarised and cannot be fitted the wrong way round, or to another type of port on the motherboard such as a Firewire type.

The case used for the demonstration PC only has two USB ports on the front panel, leaving one of the USB connectors on the motherboard unused. However, this did not go to waste as it was needed for the Flash card reader (Figure 2.64). The card reader only needs one of the USB ports, but it implements the other one via a standard USB socket to the right of the various card slots. This gives the PC a total of seven USB ports, with four in the main cluster of ports at the rear, two on the front panel, and one on the cards reader. Half a dozen or so USB ports are sufficient for most users.

It is possible that there will be other types of port available on the motherboard, such as Firewire and RS232C serial (Com) ports. Some cases have Firewire ports on the front panel together with a lead that should connect to a suitable motherboard without any difficulty. It is unlikely that the case will have connectors for anything beyond audio, USB, and Firewire ports.

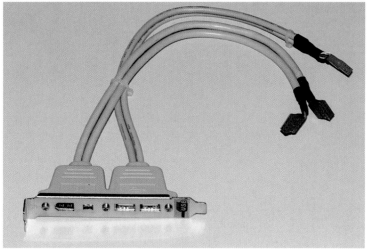

*Fig.2.65 A back-plate for addtional USB and Firewire ports*

One or two back-plates for optional ports are sometimes included with the more expensive motherboards, but it is more usual for these to be available as optional extras. The back-plate shown in Figure 2.65 has connectors for two USB ports and two different types of Firewire port. A back-plate can be used behind any unused expansion slot, and it is effectively an expansion card without the card part. When I needed an RS232C serial port on the demonstration PC I was able to implement one using a back-plate fitted with the appropriate type of connector and lead.

## Case fan

Many PC cases come complete with a cooling fan, but this is by no means a universal feature. It is definitely a good idea to fit one yourself if the fan is not included as standard. There is usually provision for a fan to be fitted on the rear and side panels, and possibly on the front section of the case as well. In terms of efficiency it probably does not matter too much which of these is used, but noise from the fan is likely to be less troublesome if it is mounted on the rear panel (Figure 2.66). PC cooling fans are available in various sizes, so make sure that you obtain one that is compatible with the case. In general, the larger the fan the better it is likely to perform.

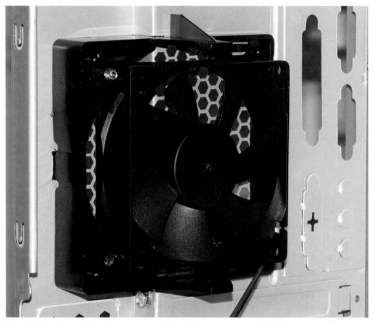

*Fig.2.66  A cooling fan mounted on the rear panel of the case.  Fans fitted on the side or front panels can be more noisy*

Some fans have a connector that enables them to be powered from the motherboard, and most motherboards have a power port for an additional fan.  Do not use the motherboard's power port for the CPU fan with a case cooling fan.  It is more usual for a case cooling fan to have a connector that enables it to be used with a 5.25-inch drive power lead. There is normally a "through" lead and connector so that the power lead can be used with a drive as well.  However, with a modern PC there are usually one or two spare power leads of this type, so the "through" feature will probably not be needed.

## Tidying up

At this point you probably have a complete PC base unit that is ready for testing.  There may be one or two other leads that need to be connected if the computer has any unusual facilities. Where necessary, add any extra cables in accordance with the instructions in manuals for the items of equipment concerned.  The exterior of the finished PC should look reasonably smart (Figure 2.67 and 2.68), but the interior of the finished PC can look a bit untidy (Figure 2.69). ATX motherboards have helped to reduce the amount of cabling in a modern PC, and the trend towards integrated features such as sound and graphics also helps reduce the amount of clutter inside a PC. On the other hand, PCs seem to become ever more complex and have more and more ports, making the clutter problem as bad as it has ever been.

Results can certainly be made much neater by fixing the cables to convenient points on the case rather than

Fig.2.67 A front view of the finished PC

just leaving them dangling. It is definitely a good idea to secure each cable in at least one place if the PC will be transported several miles or more. It is otherwise of relatively little importance. Double-sided adhesive pads represent the easiest way of fixing the cables to the case, drive bays, or whatever.

It is best not to get carried away with this sort of thing. I once bought a PC that had received a glowing review in a magazine, and it had been particularly complemented for the tidiness of its cables. The interior of the PC was indeed very neat, but there were major problems each time I tried to upgrade any of the hardware. The very neat cabling was effectively barring access to the drives, memory, expansion cards, and just about everything else inside the PC. It was necessary to carefully cut one or two cables free each time a change was made to the hardware.

Tidy up the cabling by all means, but do not get carried away to the point that upgrading or repairing the computer will be difficult.

## Testing

Before connecting the mouse, keyboard, monitor, and any peripherals such as printers, it is definitely a good idea to thoroughly check everything, making sure that all the cables are connected correctly and that none have been accidentally dislodged when working on the unit. Most of the connectors do not lock into place, and it is very easy to dislodge one connector while fitting another. Also check

*Fig.2.68  The rear of the finished PC*

that any expansion cards are fitted into their slots properly.

It is not possible to boot from the hard disc until it has been properly prepared, and an operating system has been installed. Booting from something like a MS-DOS boot disc will probably not be an option either, due to the lack of a floppy disc drive in most modern PCs. However, when the computer is switched on it should go through the normal BIOS start-up routine. By default it will probably be set to auto-detect the IDE devices, and it will probably list the drives that are detected.

*Fig.2.69  The interior of the completed PC.  Some tidying of the cables is required*

If nothing happens, or there is any sign of a malfunction, switch off at once and recheck the entire wiring, etc.  Assuming all is well, the next step is to go into the ROM BIOS Setup program and configure the CMOS memory correctly.  This is covered in the next chapter and will not be considered further here.

## Troubleshooting

Provided you proceed carefully, checking and double-checking everything as you go, and observing the basic anti-static handling precautions, you will be very unlucky indeed if the finished computer fails to start up correctly.  However meticulous you are though, there is still an outside chance that things will not go perfectly, and if you take an "it will be all right on the night" approach to things it is likely that things will be far from all right when the new PC is switched on.

This is definitely something where the old adage that "prevention is better than cure" applies. Most computer components are reasonably idiot-proof, and if an error should be made it is unlikely that any damage will occur. This possibility cannot be totally ruled out though, and there is a small but real risk of mistakes proving to be quite costly. Check everything as you go along, and then carefully recheck the finished PC before switching it on. If possible, get someone to check everything for you. Having fooled yourself into making a mistake it is easy to make the same mistake when you check the finished unit. The mistake will probably be glaringly obvious to a fresh pair of eyes.

## Blank expression

A faulty PC may start to go through the initial start-up routine and then fail at some stage, usually after the initial BIOS checks as the computer goes into the boot-up phase. Alternatively it may simply refuse to do anything, or sit there on the desk producing "beeping" noises with a blank screen. If switching on the PC results in nothing happening at all, with no sign of cooling fans operating or front panel lights switching on, the obvious first step is to check that power is getting to the computer. Is the power lead plugged in properly at both the computer and the mains outlet, and is the mains supply switched on at the outlet? It is a silly mistake to forget to plug the computer into the mains supply or to switch on the supply, but it is easily done in your haste to try out the new PC. Also check that the fuse in the mains plug is present and correct.

A PC power supply is a fairly sophisticated piece of electronics that contains numerous protection circuits. The fact that it fails to operate even though it is receiving power does not necessarily mean that it is faulty. It could simply be that a protection circuit is detecting a problem somewhere and is shutting down the supply circuit. An overload on one of the supply lines could cause this, but is not a likely cause of the problem with a new PC. However, you can not totally rule out the possibility that the cause of the problem is a fault in one of the components that the supply is powering.

A more likely cause is that the leads carrying the output of the supply are not connected properly. It is worth removing and refitting the power connector to the motherboard to make quite sure that it is fully pressed down and into place. These connectors lock into place, a connector is not fitted properly if you can free it without releasing the locking mechanism. In normal use an ATX power supply is switched on and off via a simple pushbutton switch on the front of the case, and not by way of a conventional on/off switch in the mains supply. Check that the on/off switch is connected to the motherboard correctly. Fitting the leads that connect various items on the case to the motherboard tends to be rather fiddly, and mistakes are easily made when installing these leads.

If the PC uses a motherboard that requires one or two supplementary power leads, make sure that these are both connected to the motherboard correctly. Remember that a 20-pin power connector can only be used with a 24-pin connector on the motherboard if the instruction manual states that this is acceptable.

The problem could simply be that the power supply is overloaded. As pointed out previously, the ratings of the power supplies included with budget PC cases tend to be a trifle optimistic. An overloaded power supply may not simply result in the PC refusing to start. In my experience it is more likely that the PC will start up all right but it will tend to sporadically reset or switch off for no apparent reason.

The demonstration PC suffered from this problem, with the power supply running for a short while and then cutting out. Removing the IDE DVD drive reduced the power consumption of the PC and almost cured the problem, but the supply unit still tended to switch off when the computer had been running for some time. As the original power supply was quite noisy, I was happy to replace it with a "silent" 650 watt unit that provided reliable results and a much lower low noise level that was better suited to media applications.

## Simplify

It is often possible to locate the source of the problem by simplifying the computer. In order for a PC to function it is only necessary to have one disc drive, so try totally disconnecting all the drives apart from the primary hard disc drive. If the computer still fails to start properly, disconnect the primary hard disc drive and reconnect one of the others. Try removing any non-essential expansion cards, which probably means anything other than a video card. If you have an old video card that is compatible with the expansion slot in the new PC, try using it in place of the new video card.

Expansion cards have tended to be troublesome throughout the history of the PC. Modern cards have a large number of terminals on their edge connectors, making perfect alignment of the card and the slot even more important than in the past. Fortunately, modern cards seem to be manufactured to closer tolerances than some of those from a few years ago, which seemed to be a bit approximate and did not work properly in the expansion slots of some PCs. Modern cards are much better, and should work perfectly provided they are fitted correctly. However, having the card fitted at even a very slight slant is almost certain to prevent the computer from starting.

The simplification process can usually be tried with the memory modules. Most PCs have the memory in the form of two or four memory modules, but most motherboards will work using just one module. Using a single memory module is not always acceptable though, so check this point in the motherboard's instruction manual first.

Mostly when a newly built PC fails to function properly, it actually starts up correctly and even goes through to the stage where the operating system has been installed and the computer is in use. The problem is often something quite obscure that only occurs when a particular set of circumstances exist, such as two peripheral gadgets being used simultaneously. This type of thing is usually caused by problems with the driver software for one of the pieces of hardware. The problem does not surface earlier, because it can only occur once the computer is set up properly with the operating system and all the driver software installed.

This is actually a problem that can plague any new PC, and it is not one that is specific to a home constructed PC. Updating the driver software for the relevant item or items of hardware should cure the problem. The driver software for most pieces of hardware is updated quite frequently, especially for relatively new devices. Eventually any problems are sorted out and few, if any, further updates are issued. The equipment manufacturer's web site should have the latest driver software available for all the items they produce.

Odd compatibility problems can be due to a fault in the BIOS rather than the driver software. This type of thing is very rare and you would be very unlucky indeed to experience this type of difficulty, but it does occur from time to time. The motherboard manufacturer's web site should have the latest version of the BIOS available as a download, together with the utility program needed to write it to the BIOS. There will be accompanying notes for each new version of the BIOS, and these will explain the problems each one solves. Note that in some cases the updates simply enable the motherboard to be used with new processors and do not actually solve any problems. Only update the BIOS if it will solve a specific problem. It is a slightly risky business that should not be undertaken unless it will bring real benefits.

# BIOS and operating system

## Essentials

Before you can go on to install the operating system and applications it is essential to set up the BIOS correctly. I suppose that this is not strictly true with modern PCs, where the BIOS usually auto-detects everything it needs to know, and sets sensible default values. Everything might work all right if you ignore the BIOS and move straight on to installing the operating system. However, it is still a good idea to go into the BIOS Setup program, even if it is just to check that everything is all right. It is likely that you will wish to change one or two settings.

A modern BIOS Setup program enables dozens of parameters to be controlled, many of which are highly technical. This tends to make the BIOS intimidating for those who are new to PC building, and even those who have some experience of PC construction. However, in order to get the PC running to your liking it is just a matter of adjusting a few basic parameters and perhaps doing some "fine tuning" of a few other settings. The more technical and obscure aspects of the BIOS will not be covered here, and are not something that the uninitiated should "play" with.

## BIOS basics

Before looking at the BIOS Setup program, it would perhaps be as well to consider the function of the BIOS. BIOS is an acronym and it stands for basic input/output system. Its basic function is to help the operating system handle the input and output devices, such as the drives, and ports, and also the memory circuits. It is a program that is stored in a ROM on the motherboard. These days the chip is usually quite small

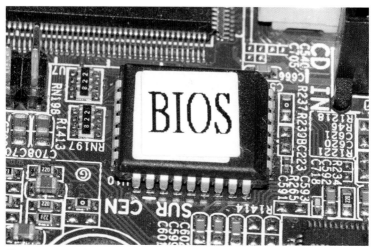

*Fig.3.1  The BIOS Setup program is contained in a chip on the
            motherboard*

(Figure 3.1), and sometimes sports a holographic label to prove that it is
the genuine article.

Because the BIOS program is in a ROM on the motherboard it can be
run immediately at start-up without the need for any form of booting
process.  It is the BIOS that runs the test routines at switch-on, or the
POST (power on self test) as it is known.  With these tests completed
successfully the BIOS then looks for an operating system to load from
disc.  The operating system appears to load itself from disc, which is a
bit like pulling oneself up by ones bootlaces.  It is said to be from this
that the term "boot" is derived.  Of course, in reality the operating system
is not loading itself initially, and it is reliant on the BIOS getting things
started.

Another role of the BIOS is to provide software routines that help the
operating system to utilize the hardware effectively.  It can also store
information about the hardware for use by the operating system, and
possibly other software.  It is this second role that makes it necessary to
have the Setup program.  The BIOS can actually detect much of the
system hardware and store the relevant technical information in memory.

However, some parameters have to be set manually, such as the time
and date, and the user may wish to override some of the default settings.
The Setup program enables the user to control the settings that the BIOS

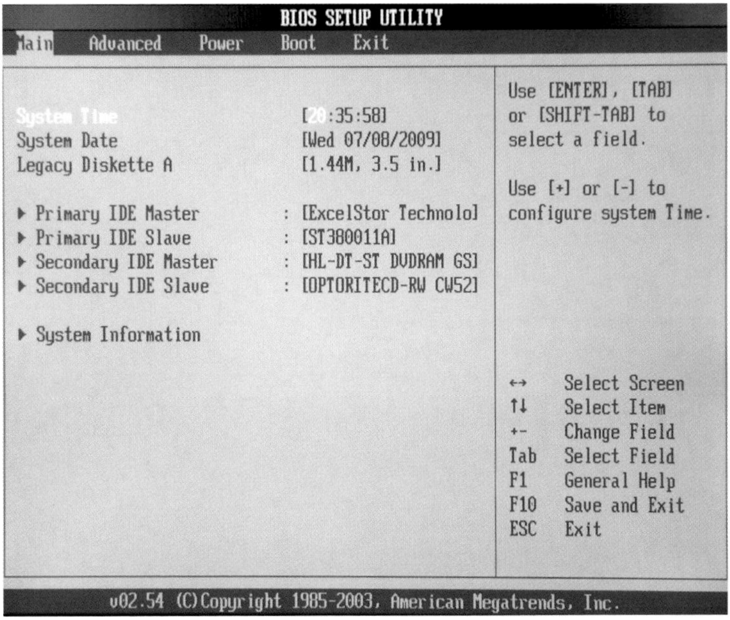

Fig.3.2  *Some versions of the AMI BIOS use tabs near the top of the screen to select the required section*

stores away in its memory. A battery powers this memory when the PC is switched off, so its contents are available each time the PC is turned on. Once you have set the correct parameters you will probably not need to deal with the BIOS Setup program again unless you do some drastic upgrading.

## Entry

In the past there have been several common means of getting into the BIOS Setup program, but with the motherboards available to amateur builders at present there is only one method in common use. This is to press the Delete key at the appropriate point during the initial testing phase just after switch-on. The BIOS will display a message, usually in the bottom left-hand corner of the screen, telling you to press the "Del" key to enter the Setup program. The instruction manual should provide details if the motherboard you are using has a different method of entering the Setup program.

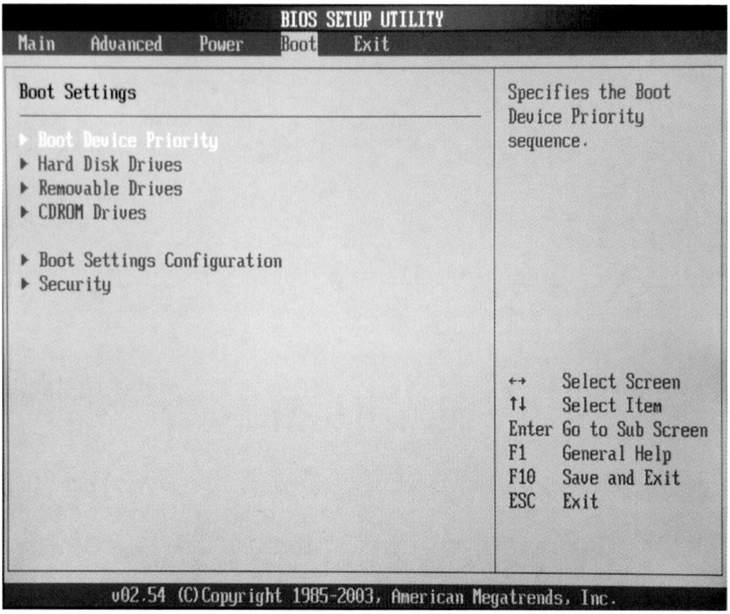

```
                         BIOS SETUP UTILITY
 Main    Advanced    Power    Boot    Exit

 Boot Settings                             Specifies the Boot
                                           Device Priority
 ▶ Boot Device Priority                    sequence.
 ▶ Hard Disk Drives
 ▶ Removable Drives
 ▶ CDROM Drives

 ▶ Boot Settings Configuration
 ▶ Security


                                           ↔      Select Screen
                                           ↑↓     Select Item
                                           Enter  Go to Sub Screen
                                           F1     General Help
                                           F10    Save and Exit
                                           ESC    Exit


           v02.54 (C)Copyright 1985-2003, American Megatrends, Inc.
```

*Fig.3.3  Here the boot section of an AMI BIOS has been selected*

The manual should also have a section dealing with the BIOS. It is worth looking through this section to determine which features can be controlled via the BIOS. Unfortunately, most motherboard instruction manuals assume the user is familiar with all the BIOS features, and there will be few detailed explanations. In fact there will probably just be a list of the available options and no real explanations at all. However, a quick read through this section of the manual will give you a good idea of what the BIOS is all about. A surprisingly large number of PC users who are quite expert in other aspects of PC operation have no real idea what the BIOS and the BIOS Setup program actually do. If you fall into this category the section of the manual that deals with the BIOS should definitely be given at least a quick read through.

There are several BIOS manufacturers and their BIOS Setup programs each work in a slightly different fashion. With motherboards available to the do-it-yourself builder it is probably the ones from Award - Phoenix, and AMI that are most likely to be encountered. At one time the AMI BIOS had a Setup program that would detect any reasonably standard mouse connected to the PC. With the aid of a mouse it offered a simple

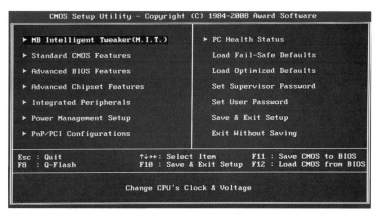

Fig.3.4  The main screen of the Award BIOS Setup program of the
        demonstration PC

form of WIMP environment, although keyboard control was still available.
This system seems to have been dropped, and a modern AMI BIOS
uses a more conventional approach with tabs at the top of the screen
providing access to the various sections of the program (Figures 3.2
and 3.3).  The required tab is selected via the keyboard and not using a
mouse.  The Award-Phoenix BIOS is probably the most common and as
far as I am aware it only uses keyboard control.  Figure 3.4 shows the
main menu for a modern Award-Phoenix BIOS.

Apart from variations in the BIOS due to different manufacturers, the
BIOS will vary slightly from one motherboard to another.  This is simply
due to the fact that features available on one motherboard may be absent
or different on another motherboard.  Also, the world of PCs in general is
developing at an amazing rate, and this is reflected in frequent BIOS
updates.  The description of the BIOS provided here has to be a
representative one, and the BIOS in your PC will inevitably be slightly
different.  The important features should be present in any BIOS, and it
is only the more minor and obscure features that are likely to be different.
The motherboard's instruction manual should at the least give some
basic information on setting up and using any unusual features.

## Standard CMOS

There are so many parameters that can be controlled via the BIOS Setup
program that they are normally divided into half a dozen or so groups.
The most important of these is the "Standard CMOS Setup" (Figure 3.5),

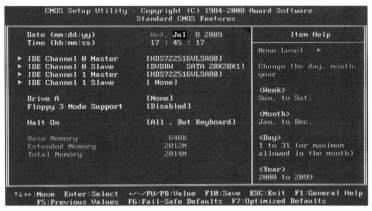

*Fig.3.5  The Standard CMOS Setup screen is an important one*

which is basically the same as the BIOS Setup in the original AT style PCs. The first parameters in the list are the time and date. These can usually be set via an operating system utility these days, but you may as well set them from the Setup program while you are in that section of the program. There are on-screen instructions that tell you how to alter and select options. One slight oddity to watch out for is that you often have to use the Page Up key to decrement values, and the Page Down key to increment them.

With virtually any modern BIOS a help screen can be brought up by pressing F1, and this used to be context sensitive. However, with a modern BIOS it usually provides some general help with using the program, and often provides little more information than is already present at the bottom of the screen (Figure 3.6). Context sensitive help is still available, but with a modern BIOS it is permanently displayed in the right-hand section of the screen.

Some of the help screens are quite large, and it is necessary to scroll down in order to see all the information. The Help panel must be made active first, and this is just a matter of pressing the F2 function key. The Up and Down cursor keys are then used to scroll the panel. It would be unrealistic to expect long explanations from a simple off-line help system, and the help provided is very brief and to the point. Use the Escape key to exit the Help panel and make the main area of the screen active again.

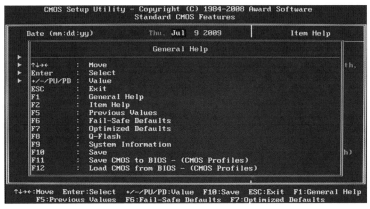

CMOS Setup Utility - Copyright (C) 1984-2008 Award Software
Standard CMOS Features

| Date (mm:dd:yy) | Thu, Jul 9 2009 | Item Help |

General Help

| ↑↓→← | : | Move |
| Enter | : | Select |
| +/-/PU/PD | : | Value |
| ESC | : | Exit |
| F1 | : | General Help |
| F2 | : | Item Help |
| F5 | : | Previous Values |
| F6 | : | Fail-Safe Defaults |
| F7 | : | Optimized Defaults |
| F8 | : | Q-Flash |
| F9 | : | System Information |
| F10 | : | Save |
| F11 | : | Save CMOS to BIOS - (CMOS Profiles) |
| F12 | : | Load CMOS from BIOS - (CMOS Profiles) |

↑↓→←:Move  Enter:Select  +/-/PU/PD:Value  F10:Save  ESC:Exit  F1:General Help
F5:Previous Values  F6:Fail-Safe Defaults  F7:Optimized Defaults

*Fig.3.6  The general Help screen is not all that helpful*

## Drive settings

In days gone by, the next section would have been used to set the operating parameters for the drives on the IDE ports. Really all you have to do here with a modern PC is check that all the drives have been found and identified correctly. The parallel IDE DVD drive originally fitted to the demonstration PC had been removed by the time the screen shot of Figure 3.5 was taken, so the BIOS has correctly identified the complement of drives as two SATA hard discs and one SATA DVD drive. It is still possible to set the drive parameters manually (Figure 3.7), but it is probably only worthwhile doing so if the instruction manual for the drive recommends this method and provides the correct parameters for the drive.

Note that any "drives" that are actually Flash card readers/writers will not be found and listed by the BIOS. However, they should still be found and used correctly by the operating system. There is a problem if virtually the opposite of this occurs, with a floppy disc drive being listed even though no drive of this type has been installed. By default, the BIOS will sometimes include a floppy drive regardless of whether one is actually present, and this can even "fool" the operating system into including floppy drive A in the list of available drives. Change the setting to "None" if a phantom floppy is listed by the BIOS.

The next section is used to determine the course of action taken by the BIOS if an error is detected during the POST. The default setting is usually

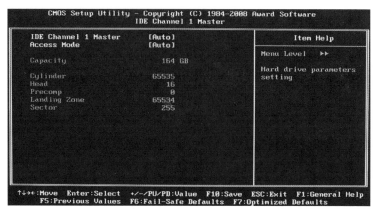

Fig.3.7  If necessary, the drive parameters can be set manually

for any error, apart from a keyboard type, to halt the system and prevent the computer from booting into the operating system. This avoids having a faulty system corrupt the hard disc drive, possibly damaging the operating system and important data in the process. A keyboard error is unlikely to cause any major problems if the computer is allowed to boot into the operating system. Most keyboard errors are of the "stuck keys" variety, and are usually caused by someone leaning on the keyboard or leaving something on it, rather than by a genuinely faulty keyboard.

With a modern BIOS the amount of memory is automatically detected and entered into the CMOS RAM. The "Standard CMOS Setup" screen will report the amount of memory fitted, so you do not need to set this parameter manually, and it is unlikely that there will be any way of altering this setting manually. You should obviously check that the displayed figure actually matches the amount of memory installed on the motherboard. It there is a discrepancy it is virtually certain that the BIOS is correctly indicating the amount of memory that is installed properly. The most likely cause of the problem is that one of the memory modules is not fitted properly, or has been fitted in the wrong memory slot.

## BIOS Settings

Another section of the BIOS Setup program that should be checked is the one called something like BIOS Settings or Advanced BIOS Settings. This produces a screen that should look similar to the one shown in Figure 3.8. The important thing here is the order of the boot drives. The

```
           CMOS Setup Utility - Copyright (C) 1984-2008 Award Software
                           Advanced BIOS Features
  ► Hard Disk Boot Priority      [Press Enter]            Item Help
    First Boot Device            [CDROM]
    Second Boot Device           [Hard Disk]        Menu Level    ►
    Third Boot Device            [Disabled]
    Password Check               [Setup]            Select Hard Disk Boot
    HDD S.M.A.R.T. Capability    [Enabled]          Device Priority.
    Limit CPUID Max. to 3        [Disabled]
    No-Execute Memory Protect    [Enabled]
    CPU Enhanced Halt (C1E)      [Enabled]
    C2/C2E State Support         [Disabled]
    CPU Thermal Monitor 2(TM2)   [Enabled]
    CPU EIST Function            [Enabled]
    Delay For HDD (Secs)         [ 0]




  ↑↓→←:Move   Enter:Select   +/-/PU/PD:Value   F10:Save   ESC:Exit   F1:General Help
             F5:Previous Values   F6:Fail-Safe Defaults   F7:Optimized Defaults
```

*Fig.3.8   This section of the BIOS Setup program is used to set the boot sequence*

BIOS used to check the floppy disc drive for a boot disc first, and then go on to the hard drive if no floppy boot disc was found.  With most new PCs no longer having a floppy disc drive it is usually necessary to arrange things differently.  Modern operating systems are installed from a CD-ROM, or a DVD.  In the case of Windows XP, Vista, and 7, it is normally a DVD that is used.  In order to install the operating system it is necessary to boot from the Windows installation disc in the CD or DVD drive.

This is not usually possible if the computer is set to boot from the hard disc drive first, and then from the CD/DVD drive if the hard disc is not bootable. Ideally this would happen, but in practice the computer tends to come to a halt if it tries to boot from a hard disc drive that does not contain an operating system.  Initially anyway, it is therefore important to have the CD/DVD drive as the first bootable device, and the hard disc drive as the second bootable device.

It is important to realise that simply having the operating system installation disc in the CD/DVD drive is not usually sufficient to make the computer use it as the boot disc even if the CD/DVD drive is set as the primary boot device.  There is usually an onscreen prompt at the appropriate time, and pressing any key of the keyboard will then result in the computer booting from the installation disc.  This may seem to be an unnecessary complication, but it avoids problems when the computer reboots during the installation process.

A Windows installation usually requires at least a couple of reboots, and there is a potential problem in that the computer must not reboot from the installation CD/DVD. Numerous files are written to the hard disc drive during the initial stages of installation, and it is these files that must be used when the computer reboots during the installation process. This could result in an unattended PC just going through the initial stages of installation indefinitely.

However, this does not happen if it is necessary to press a key in order to boot from the CD/DVD drive. The user must press the key in order to start the installation process, but they do not have to watch over the computer while the main installation is carried out. When the computer reboots it will not boot from the installation disc because no one will press a key of the keyboard, so it will instead move on to the second boot disc, which must be the hard disc drive.

Anyway, in order to make installation of the operating system as straightforward as possible, make sure that the CD/DVD drive is set as the first boot device, and that the hard disc drive is set as the second boot device. The assignment of any further boot drives is not important since any third or fourth boot devices will not be reached. You might prefer to have the hard disc drive as the primary boot device once the operating system has been installed, and doing so will slightly speed up the boot process. However, remember that it will be necessary to set the CD/DVD drive as the first boot device again if it should be necessary to reinstall or upgrade the operating system, or boot from this drive for another reason, such as when using a bootable antivirus rescue disc.

## Integrated Peripherals

The Integrated Peripherals section (Figure 3.9) provides some control over the on-board interfaces. In particular, it allows some ports to be switched on or off, and in the case of any serial or parallel ports it will enable the port addresses and interrupt (IRQ) numbers to be altered. This can be useful when trying to avoid conflicts with hardware fitted in the expansion slots, but is unlikely to be necessary with a modern PC. The number of integrated peripherals on current motherboards is such that the options in this section of the BIOS will largely be handled by sub-menus.

An important thing to check in this section is that any on-board ports that you will be using, other than those in the main cluster at the rear of the PC, are actually switched on. The ports in the main cluster are permanently enabled, but the additional ports such as serial (COM), Firewire, and USB types will not necessarily be switched on by default.

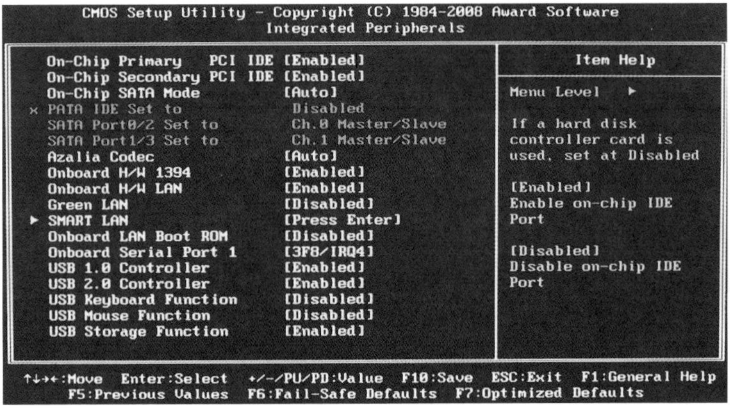

```
         CMOS Setup Utility - Copyright (C) 1984-2008 Award Software
                           Integrated Peripherals

    On-Chip Primary   PCI IDE [Enabled]              │        Item Help
    On-Chip Secondary PCI IDE [Enabled]              │
    On-Chip SATA Mode         [Auto]                 │ Menu Level    ▶
  × PATA IDE Set to           Disabled               │
    SATA Port0/2 Set to       Ch.0 Master/Slave      │ If a hard disk
    SATA Port1/3 Set to       Ch.1 Master/Slave      │ controller card is
    Azalia Codec              [Auto]                 │ used, set at Disabled
    Onboard H/W 1394          [Enabled]              │
    Onboard H/W LAN           [Enabled]              │ [Enabled]
    Green LAN                 [Disabled]             │ Enable on-chip IDE
  ▶ SMART LAN                 [Press Enter]          │ Port
    Onboard LAN Boot ROM      [Disabled]             │
    Onboard Serial Port 1     [3F8/IRQ4]             │ [Disabled]
    USB 1.0 Controller        [Enabled]              │ Disable on-chip IDE
    USB 2.0 Controller        [Enabled]              │ Port
    USB Keyboard Function     [Disabled]             │
    USB Mouse Function        [Disabled]             │
    USB Storage Function      [Enabled]              │

 ↑↓→←:Move  Enter:Select  +/-/PU/PD:Value  F10:Save  ESC:Exit  F1:General Help
        F5:Previous Values  F6:Fail-Safe Defaults  F7:Optimized Defaults
```

*Fig.3.9  This section provides control over some of the interfaces*

It can be useful to enable the USB keyboard and mouse functions. These are not needed by the operating system or the BIOS in order to use a USB keyboard and mouse, but they are sometimes needed when installing the operating system. They can be switched off again once the operating system has been installed.

## Power Management

Most operating systems and all modern motherboards seem to support some form of power management facility. In other words, the computer goes into some form of standby mode if there is no mouse or keyboard activity for a certain period. Most motherboards can also be switched to and from a standby mode via a peripheral such as a modem, and this also comes under the general heading of power management. A modern BIOS usually has a section dealing solely with power management (Figure 3.10).

With a modern PC, power management is a feature that is largely controlled by the operating system. Therefore, most changes to the power management settings are made by way of the operating system rather than the BIOS. This section of the BIOS can probably be ignored, and is only needed if you wish to alter something that cannot be adjusted via the operating system.

```
        CMOS Setup Utility - Copyright (C) 1984-2008 Award Software
                            Power Management Setup
┌──────────────────────────────────────────────┬──────────────────────────┐
│  ACPI Suspend Type        [S3(STR)]           │        Item Help         │
│  Soft-Off by PWR-BTTN     [Instant-Off]       │                          │
│  PME Event Wake Up        [Enabled]           │  Menu Level    ►         │
│  Power On by Ring         [Enabled]           │                          │
│  Resume by Alarm          [Disabled]          │  [S1(POS)]               │
│ x Date(of Month) Alarm      Everyday          │  Set suspend type to     │
│ x Time(hh:mm:ss) Alarm      0 :  0 :  0       │  Power On Suspend under  │
│  HPET Support             [Enabled]           │  ACPI OS                 │
│  HPET Mode                [32-bit mode]       │                          │
│  Power On By Mouse        [Disabled]          │  [S3(STR)]               │
│  Power On By Keyboard     [Disabled]          │  Set suspend type to     │
│ x KB Power ON Password      Enter             │  Suspend to RAM under    │
│  AC Back Function         [Soft-Off]          │  ACPI OS                 │
│                                               │                          │
│                                               │                          │
│                                               │                          │
│                                               │                          │
├──────────────────────────────────────────────┴──────────────────────────┤
│ ↑↓→←:Move  Enter:Select  +/-/PU/PD:Value  F10:Save  ESC:Exit  F1:General Help │
│       F5:Previous Values  F6:Fail-Safe Defaults  F7:Optimized Defaults        │
└──────────────────────────────────────────────────────────────────────────┘
```

Fig.3.10   There is a Power Management section, but this aspect of the
          PC is usually controlled via the operating system

## PC Health Status

Most motherboards now support at least a basic over-temperature
detection circuit for the processor, and there are often various CPU
threshold temperatures that can be selected. Figure 3.11 shows the PC
Health Status screen of the BIOS used in the demonstration PC. This
screen provides both temperature and voltage monitoring, and
additionally it monitors the cooling fans. As a minimum, the PC Health
Status screen should show the system temperature (the temperature
inside the PC's case) and the processor's temperature. Typically, this
example also shows various operating voltages. If the CPU goes above
the selected temperature a warning can be produced, and the PC usually
shuts down as well. It is probably best to activate this feature and simply
leave the threshold temperature at its default setting.

The normal operating temperature varies considerably from one type of
processor to another. In general, the processor should operate below
about 50 degrees Celsius, but some chips seem to operate quite happily
at around 60 degrees, while others settle down at around 40 degrees or
even less. Unless you know what you are doing it is not a good idea to
alter the default alarm temperatures. Note that many motherboards are
supplied complete with so-called health monitoring software that enables
parameters such as the CPU temperature, fan speeds, operating voltages,
etc., to be monitored while running Windows. It is well worthwhile
installing any bundled software of this type.

```
       CMOS Setup Utility - Copyright (C) 1984-2008 Award Software
                             PC Health Status

   Reset Case Open Status      [Disabled]                Item Help
   Case Opened                 Yes
   Vcore                       1.204U             Menu Level   ▶
   DDR18U                      1.936U
   +3.3U                       3.376U             [Disabled]
   +12U                       12.556U             Don't reset case
   Current System Temperature   37°C              open status
   Current CPU Temperature      39°C
   Current CPU FAN Speed        949 RPM           [Enabled]
   Current SYSTEM FAN Speed    1493 RPM           Clear case open status
   CPU Warning Temperature    [60°C/140°F]        and set to be Disabled
   CPU FAN Fail Warning       [Enabled]           at next boot
   SYSTEM FAN Fail Warning    [Enabled]
   CPU Smart FAN Control      [Enabled]




 ↑↓→←:Move  Enter:Select  +/-/PU/PD:Value  F10:Save  ESC:Exit  F1:General Help
       F5:Previous Values  F6:Fail-Safe Defaults  F7:Optimized Defaults
```

*Fig.3.11  The PC Health Status section enables various temperatures and voltages to be monitored*

Whether monitoring via the BIOS or a Windows program, do not be surprised if the measured voltages are very slightly different to the nominal voltages. There is a tolerance of plus and minus 5 percent or more on most voltages, and the measuring circuits will produce small errors that effectively widen the tolerance ratings.

The section that monitors the cooling fans will usually give the speed of rotation for each one rather than simply reporting it as working or inoperative. Note that a fan can only be monitored if it is powered from a fan output on the motherboard, and the fan is a type that has the third connection needed for monitoring purposes. With a modern PC the processor's fan should always be of this type. The system fan will not be monitored if it is a type that is powered from a 5.25-inch drive power lead. Monitoring for the system fan should be switched off if the fan is not actually being monitored. This avoids the possibility of spurious alarms or error messages being produced by the monitoring system.

Many motherboards support so-called "smart" operation of the cooling fans. This is where the speed of a fan is increased and decreased in sympathy with changes in the temperature of the system or the processor. The idea is to have the fans operate at the slowest speed commensurate with keeping the system and the processor at safe temperatures. This can be important if the computer will be used for media applications where it is desirable for the fans to make as little noise as possible. It is otherwise best to switch off this feature so that the fans always operate at full speed, and everything is kept as cool as possible.

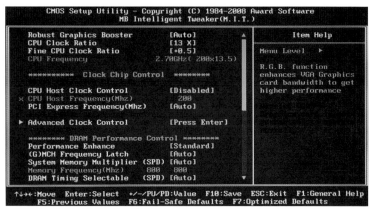

*Fig.3.12   This section is strictly for those who know what they are doing*

## Over-clocking

Although it is by no means a universal feature, it is quite common for the BIOS to have a section that enables some parameters, such as the clock speed of the processor, to be "fine tuned" (Figure 3.12). The idea is to get the computer to go as fast as possible without compromising reliability. However, this type of thing relies on running the processor and other parts of the system beyond their rated limits. This could cause overheating and problems with long-term reliability, so it is something that is strictly for those who know exactly what they are doing, and who also understand the risks involved.

## Operating system

With the PC built and any necessary adjustments made to the BIOS, it is time to install the operating system. Falling hardware prices have not been matched by similar falls in software prices, and you could actually pay more for the operating system than you paid for the computer hardware. There are two basic options if the cheapest possible operating system is required. One is to use the operating system from the PC that the new one will be replacing. This does, of course, assume that the new computer will replace an old PC which will be scrapped, and that the old PC is equipped with a worthwhile operating system.

The old operating system will probably be a worthwhile proposition provided it is a version of Windows XP or Vista, but using any earlier form of Windows is unlikely to be a practical proposition. Using modern hardware with an obsolete operating system such as Windows ME is not usually possible due to the lack of suitable driver software for the hardware. Things like the soundcard, video system, and even much of the hardware on the motherboard will not function unless supported by the correct driver software.

Unfortunately, it is not safe to assume that the Windows XP or Vista operating system from an old PC can be successfully transferred to a new PC. There should be no major problem provided the operating system is either a retail type or a normal OEM (original equipment manufacturer) version. These have the standard installation disc and can be installed in the normal way.

Some PCs, and particularly those from the larger manufacturers, are supplied with a bundled version of Windows that will not run on another PC. The computer's BIOS chip contains a pass code, and the operating system will only run if it finds this code. Since the pass code will not be found if the software is used on another PC, the operating system will refuse to load. While this restriction might seem to be a little unreasonable, bear in mind that the cost of bundled versions of Windows is relatively low, and the restrictions placed on the software are simply a reflection of this fact.

Linux is now available in a few hundred variations, some of which are free, but it is also on offer in normal commercial forms. The free versions usually have little or no customer support, but usually include a wide range of application programs. In any commercial form there should be proper support from the manufacturer, and in general there are more and better application programs as well.

At one time it was often quite difficult to get Linux installed correctly and running as it should. Life is generally much easier with any of the modern versions that are intended for general use, which includes all the popular versions such as SUSE, Ubuntu, and Fedora. Even so, it is probably slightly more difficult to install than modern versions of Windows, and it can be very difficult to sort things out if the installation goes seriously awry. A modern distribution of Linux still represents a good choice for anyone aiming to produce a working PC at a "rock-bottom" price, not the least because there is usually an impressive array of free application software. Bear in mind though, that Windows programs cannot be used with Linux.

Of course, if you are prepared to pay the price, these days it is possible to buy a retail-boxed version of Windows from practically any computer software shop. Installing a retail version of Windows should be

*Fig.3.13  This screen is used to select the right language*

straightforward with "no strings attached". Do not overlook the possibility of using an OEM (original equipment manufacturer) version of Windows. These are intended for resale with new PCs, but some of the larger computer hardware and software retailers sell them at significantly lower prices than the retail versions. In order to stay within the rules it is usually necessary to buy an item of hardware together with an OEM operating system. Apparently Microsoft's rules state that OEM operating systems must be sold with hardware, rather than stipulating that they must be supplied with a complete PC. Anyway, an OEM version can cost much less than the retail equivalent, but the two are essentially the same and are installed in the same way.

## Installation options

Here we will concentrate on installing Windows, which is the operating system that most people choose for a new PC. Installing some earlier versions of Windows involved a fair amount of preamble when the hard disc drive was new, or for some other reason was blank. With a modern version of Windows the installation process is relatively simple, and is very similar whether the operating system is installed from scratch or on

*Fig.3.14  It is normally the Install Now option that is selected here.  Use the Repair option if you need to make an existing Windows installation usable with the new PC*

top of an existing Windows installation.  It is therefore largely the same whether you use a new hard disc drive or one rescued from your previous PC.

If Windows is already on the hard disc it will be detected by the Setup program, which can then reinstall Windows on top of the existing installation.  Unfortunately, simply using the existing Windows installation on a new PC is unlikely to work.  This is mainly due to the installed drivers for the old hardware not being suitable for the new hardware.  Windows will try to install the right drivers, and it might actually be able to do so.  However, this process can take longer than reinstalling Windows on top of the old installation, and it often seems to produce a rather slow version of Windows that works, but only just.  In some cases it proves to be impossible to get an old Windows installation to work at all on a new PC.

Note that the versions of Windows supplied with some PCs do not have the standard installation disc.  The methods described here are only applicable if you have the standard Windows installation disc.  Such a disc is included when you buy the retail or OEM version of Vista.  It is Windows Vista that is installed in this example, but the process is essentially the same for Windows XP, Vista, and 7.

*Fig.3.15  The product key should be entered in the textbox*

## Booting from DVD

Whether reinstalling on top of an existing installation or installing Windows Vista from scratch, the first step is to boot from the installation DVD.  As explained previously, the BIOS must be set to boot from the DVD drive before it tries to boot from the hard disc.  If all is well, a message will appear on the screen indicating that any key must be operated in order to boot from the DVD drive.  This message appears quite briefly, so be ready to press one of the keys.  The computer will try to boot from the hard disc if you "miss the boat".  It will then be necessary to restart the computer and try again.

After various files have been loaded from the DVD, things should come to a halt with the screen of Figure 3.13.  Here you use the three menus to set the installation language, the time and currency format, and the keyboard language or type.  For a UK user these are normally set at English, English (United Kingdom), and United Kingdom respectively. Operating the Next button moves things on to the screen of Figure 3.14, where the "Install now" option should be selected.  The Repair option is used if you wish to try updating an old Windows installation to run on the new PC.  This is basically just a matter of selecting the Windows installation you wish to repair, and then going through the normal

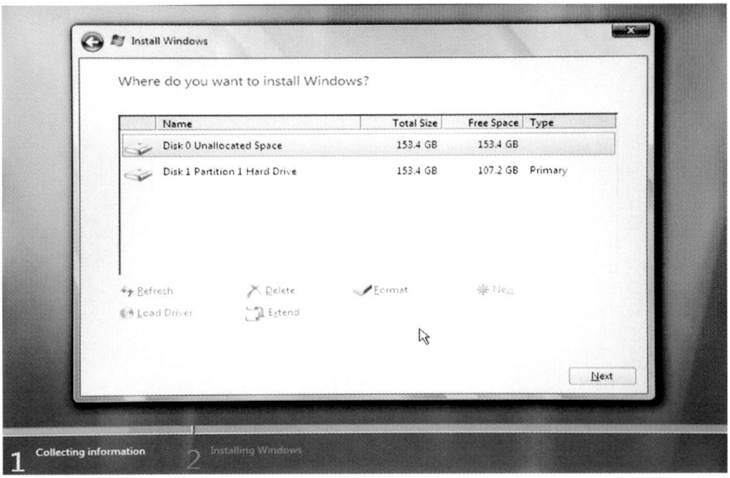

*Fig.3.16  This screen shows the available drives for installation*

installation process, and it is something that will not be considered further here.

At the following screen (Figure 3.15) you have the option of entering your product key. It is not essential to do so at this stage, but it is definitely a good idea to do so. It is also a good idea to opt for automatic activation by leaving the checkbox ticked. If the next screen provides a list of Windows versions, use it to select the version of Vista that you have purchased, and then tick the checkbox.

The Next screen will probably be the usual licence agreement, and you have to tick the checkbox in order to agree with the licensing terms. Note that Windows cannot be installed unless you do agree to the licensing conditions. At the next screen you might have the choice of upgrading an existing Windows installation or installing a fresh one, but the upgrade option is unlikely to be active. This does not matter, because it is the "Custom (advanced)" option that is required in this case.

The available disc drives are listed at the next screen (Figure 3.16), where you select the drive that will be used for the Windows Vista installation. In this example it will be installed on Disk 0 Partition 1, which at this stage is totally blank. Disk 1 has been partitioned and formatted in the old PC, and the contents of the hard disc in the old PC have been copied onto it. The new PC will therefore have all my data files ready for use on the second hard disc drive, which requires no further processing here.

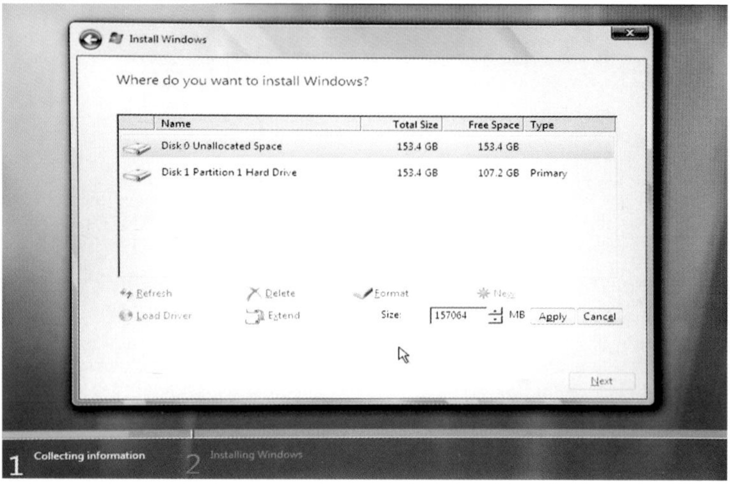

Fig.3.17  Use the default setting if a single partition will be used

In fact it is important not to accidentally reformat it or alter the partitioning, as this would almost certainly result in all the data on the disc being destroyed!

If Windows is already present on the first hard disc drive, but you wish to ignore this installation and reinstall Windows from scratch, one option is to go ahead and install the fresh copy of Windows on this partition. This will produce a warning message explaining that the files associated with the existing Windows installation will be moved to a folder called Windows.old, but the old version of Windows and the installed programs will not be usable.  You might prefer to do things this way provided the hard disc drive is large enough to take the old files and the new installation. Unwanted files can be deleted once the new installation is in place and fully operational.

There is an easier approach if any existing operating system and data on the disc is not required, and Windows will be installed "from scratch". The quick way to obliterate the entire contents of disc is to reformat it, and this is done in the same way as formatting the disc for the first time, as described later in this chapter.  Bear in mind though, that reformatting will effectively erase everything on the disc, including any data.  If you wish to retain the data files on the disc, Windows must be installed without reformatting it.  The Repair option mentioned previously is probably the best approach if you need to largely retain the contents of the hard drive.

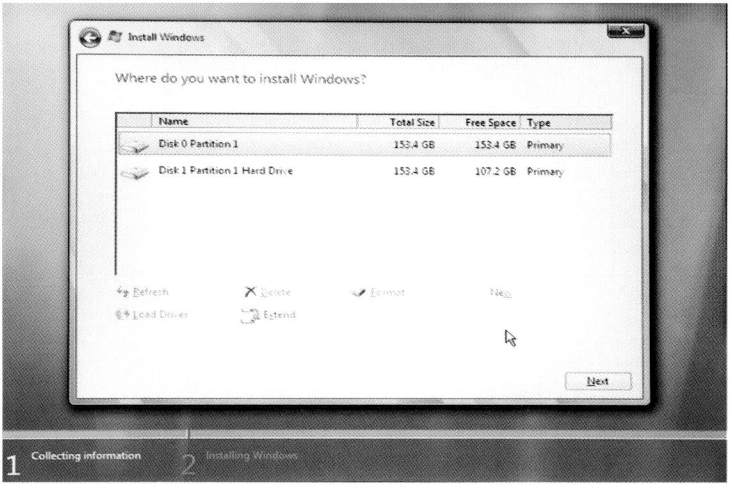

*Fig.3.18  The partition has been created successfully*

## Partitioning

When using a totally new disc there is some work to do before Windows can be installed. In order to use the disc it must have at least one partition, and the partition or partitions must be formatted. The first task is to create the required partition or partitions. In this example we will settle for one partition, and the first step is to operate the New link in the bottom of section of the window. The screen then changes, with a textbox appearing in the lower section of the screen (Figures 3.17). Simply leave this unchanged if you wish to have a single partition on the disc that is as large as possible. If more than one partition is required, enter the size required for the first one. The size of the partition is specified in megabytes, and there are 1024 megabytes per gigabyte. In this example I simply opted for the default setting as a single large partition was required.

This partition was created successfully (Figure 3.18). If a second partition is required, it is produced by selecting the unallocated disc space and repeating the procedure. It is not essential to accept the default size and use all the remaining space for the second partition. As before, a smaller size can be specified leaving space for a third partition. Dividing a disc into three separate partitions can have advantages, but bear in mind that

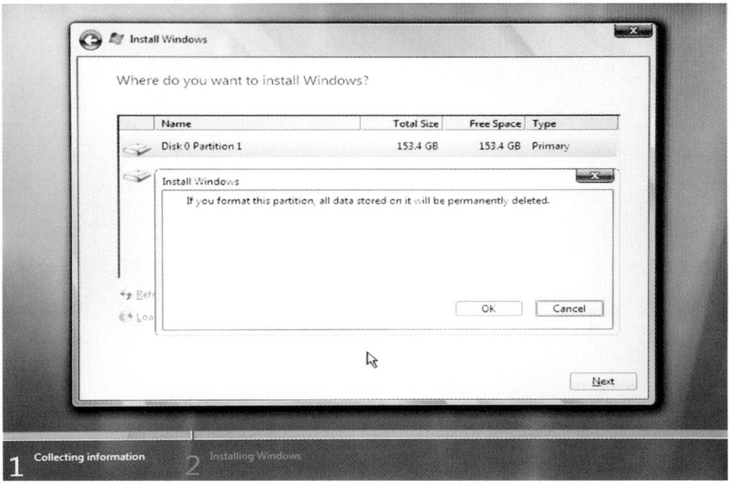

Fig.3.19  *You are warned that all data in the partition will be erased*

it can also be inefficient and inconvenient in some circumstances. Do not partition a disc in this way just for the sake of it. Only do so if you have a good reason to do so.

The disc now has a partition, but a partition is not usable until it has been formatted. Start by selecting the partition and operating the Format link. This will produce a warning message (Figure 3.19) pointing out that any data on the partition will be erased by the formatting, but in this case there is no data to lose. However, make sure that the right partition is selected in cases where there is a partition that contains data. Having formatted the first partition, repeat the process to format any other new partitions. Things do not look any different back at the main window (Figure 3.20), but the disc is now ready for the Windows installation to proceed.

## Installation

Operating the Next button moves things on to the beginning of the installation process (Figure 3.21). The screen will change to show a list of tasks, and each one will be ticked as it is completed. Installation of a modern operating system takes a fair amount of time, so be prepared to wait several minutes while various tasks are performed. The computer will be restarted at least once during installation (Figure 3.22), and as

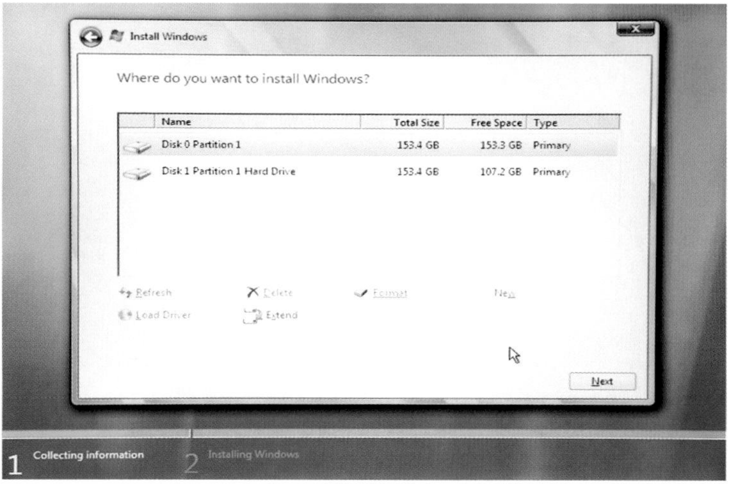

*Fig.3.20  Things look the same, but the partition has been formatted*

explained previously, it is important that it is allowed to boot from the hard disc drive when this happens.  Do not get it to boot from the installation DVD, or you will just end up going through the same steps over and over again with installation never being completed.

*Fig.3.21  The largely automatic installation process has finally started*

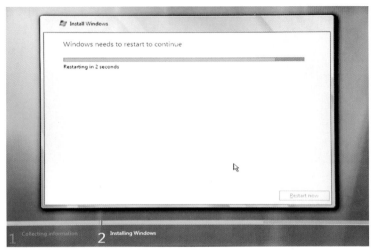

*Fig.3.22  The computer will automatically reboot at least twice*

*Fig.3.23  Choose a picture to represent your user account*

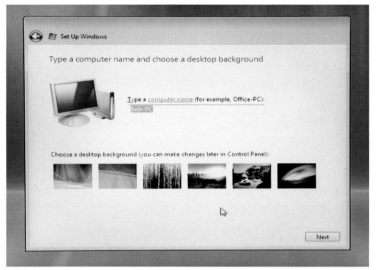

*Fig.3.24  Enter a name for the computer or just use the default name*

Although the installation process is largely automatic, it is still necessary for the user to enter some simple information during the later stages. When the screen of Figure 3.23 appears, you have to select a picture to represent your account, and supply a name for your account.  It is not essential to use password protection, but it is probably best to do so.  As usual, you will have to enter your choice of password into one textbox and then confirm that it is correct by entering it again in another textbox. An optional hint can be entered in another textbox, and the hint should be something that will help you to remember the password if you should happen to forget it.  Bear in mind that you will be locked out of your account if you forget your password and do not manage to remember it.

The next screen (Figure 3.24) is used to enter a name for the computer, or the default name can be used.  Do not confuse the account name and the computer name.  The name for the computer is the one that will be used to identify it if the computer is connected to a network.  This name must therefore be different to the names used for any other computers on the network.  It does not matter too much what name is used if the computer will not be used as part of a network.  The account name given at the previous screen is the one used for your account on the computer. Other accounts can be added once Windows is installed and running

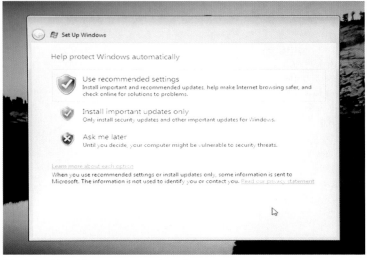

*Fig.3.25  Use this screen to select the type of updates to be installed*

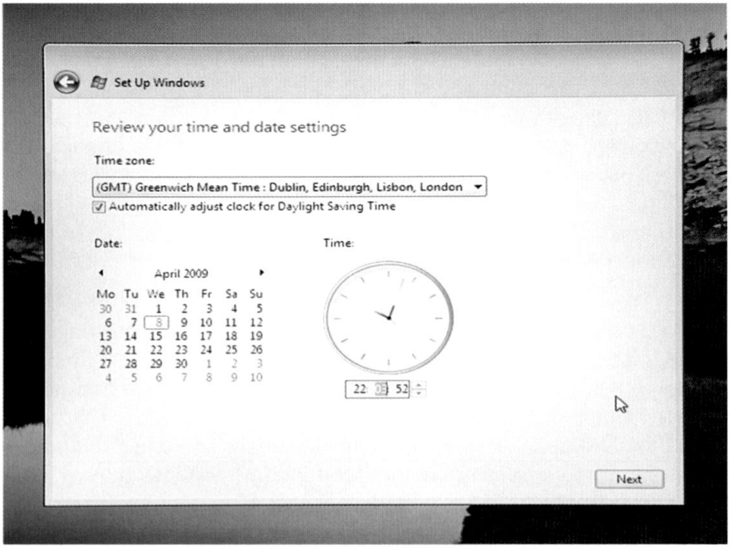

*Fig.3.26  Use this screen to set the time, date, and time zone*

properly, but this is not mandatory. The general idea is to have a different account for each user, so there is usually no point in having more than one account if there is only one user.

This screen is also used to select a background design for the Windows desktop. The first design in the row of

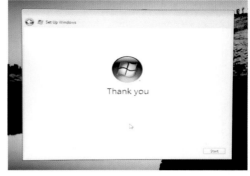

*Fig.3.27 No further input is required from the user*

thumbnail images will be used if you do not select one. Of course, the desktop's background is easily changed to just about anything you like once Windows has been installed, so it does not matter too much which design is chosen at this stage.

There are three options at the following screen (Figure 3.25), which is where you opt to have recommended updates installed, important

*Fig.3.28 This is one of various information screens that will appear*

*Fig.3.29  Finally, the computer has booted into the new Windows installation*

updates installed, or neither at this stage. It is probably best to opt for at least important updates to be installed, but the automatic update settings can be altered once Windows is installed, so there is no need to make a final decision at this stage.

The next screen (Figure 3.26) allows the time, date, and time zone to be altered, if necessary. With a new motherboard in use it is unlikely that the existing settings will be correct, and this screen provides an opportunity to make any necessary adjustments. Tick the checkbox if you wish to have Windows automatically adjust the system clock for daylight saving time. Next you might have to select from Home, Business, or Public Location, depending on where the computer will mainly be used.

The setting up procedure is now finished, which will be confirmed by the screen of Figure 3.27. Operating the Start button results in a series of information screens appearing, such as the example of Figure 3.28, while the installation is finalised. The usual log-on screen will then appear if you opted to use a password. Log-on in the usual way, and the Windows desktop (Figure 3.29) should then be obtained. The desktop will appear straight away if no password was entered during the setting up procedure. Of course, it is just the bare desktop that is obtained when Windows is installed from scratch. In order to get the computer into full working

*Fig.3.30   The motherboard is often suppied complete with a utility
program that can install the supplied drivers and possibly
some other supporting software as well*

order it is necessary to install all the application software, set the required
video resolution, customise the Windows environment, copy your data
files to the hard disc drive, etc.

With Windows installed it is a good idea to use Windows Explorer to
check that any extra hard discs and partitions are present and correct.
Writing a few test files to additional partitions and discs should confirm
that they are functioning correctly.  It is worth noting that Windows has
facilities for partitioning and formatting hard disc drives, so it is only
necessary to produce one partition during the installation process.  If
preferred, any others can be added once Windows has been installed.

## Finishing off

Having installed Windows it is unlikely that it will be fully operational and
genuinely ready to use.  The Windows installation disc might have all the
required driver software for the hardware used in the new PC, but this is
unlikely.  The newer and more "up to the minute" the hardware in your
new PC, the lower the chances of the optimum driver software being
installed right from the start by the Windows installation program.  Generic
drivers will almost certainly have been installed for some of the hardware.

These drivers might actually work quite well, but they will not get the best results from the hardware, and in some cases they only provide very limited functionality. There might even be no drivers at all for some of the hardware, which will leave it in an unusable state until suitable drivers are installed.

The motherboard should come complete with a disc that contains all the drivers needed for the hardware on the motherboard, including the integrated sound and video where appropriate. It might be necessary to install the drivers manually, but it is far more likely that there will be an installation program that largely automates the process, such as the example shown in Figure 3.30. The instruction manual for the motherboard should give detailed instructions for installing the driver software. Any additional items of hardware such as PCI expansion cards or USB devices should be supplied complete with supporting driver software, and instructions for installing it. Note that driver software is not always installed using the standard Windows method. Use the methods of installation described in the instruction manuals even if it differs from the standard Windows approach to things.

Everything should work well once the proper drivers have been installed, but there could still be some work to do. Windows is updated quite frequently, and there will probably be some updates to install. This is done using the Windows Update facility in the usual manner, but it could take much longer than normal due to a large number of updates being required. With the demonstration PC it was necessary to download and install over 70 updates, followed by a 250 megabyte service pack! There could also be updated drivers available for some of the hardware. However, unless a problem is experienced with an item of hardware it is probably not worthwhile downloading and installing a newer version of the driver software. A "let well alone" approach to things is usually the best one with driver software.

The same is true of the BIOS. Any modern PC BIOS can be updated using a simple utility program and the new data file for the BIOS. When a new BIOS file is available it can be downloaded from the web site of the motherboard's manufacturer, together with the utility program needed to install it. However, this type of upgrade is a slightly risky process that should only be undertaken if there is a definite problem that the new BIOS will cure.

# Index